Christmas Movie

ULTIMATE
TRIVIA
BOOK

Christmas Movie

ULTIMATE **TRIVIA** BOOK

Neal E. Fischer

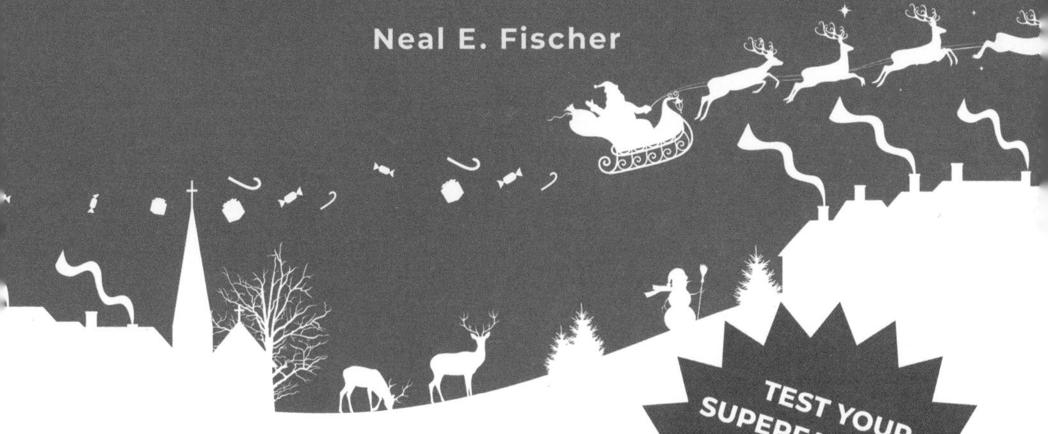

TEST YOUR SUPERFAN STATUS AND RELIVE THE MOST ICONIC CHRISTMAS MOVIE MOMENTS

EPIC INK

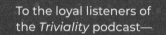

To the loyal listeners of
the *Triviality* podcast—

For seven years you've listened to
my long-winded and pop-culture-
packed questions . . . and now you
get to read them too! Thank you
for all your support. You're truly
the cream of the crop.

Contents

Introduction

I remember every Christmas of my childhood vividly. Filled with anticipation on Christmas Eve, I barely slept, only to be shaken awake at an ungodly hour by my brother. Together, we'd race down the stairs in our pjs, rush past our stockings, and dive for the presents.

Every year, we had traditions like finding the Christmas pickle ornament in the tree and visiting Santa at the mall for a picture. We'd have a family party where the cookies were plentiful, Grandma's ham was crispy with a brown sugar and dry mustard glaze, and the entire family got a scratch-off lottery ticket during dessert in the hopes one of us would win the big one to share with everyone else. I never realized as a kid just how much my parents and grandparents sacrificed to guarantee we had an amazing Christmas. I didn't find out until this year that my mom was part of a covert group that would go to multiple stores at 5:00 a.m., wait in line in the cold, and then wrestle whoever stood in their path *Jingle All the Way*–style to get all the hottest toys. Then they'd meet back at a neutral location to take stock and trade so everyone's kid woke up happy on Christmas. Can you picture a half-dozen perms in starter jackets marching into Target to grab Saba the Talking Tiger Saber by any means necessary? Where's Marty Scorsese to make that movie?

The point of all this is to let you know that I know Christmas. I know Christmas and I love Christmas. I love Christmas so much that I feel it in my fingers and my toes, and there's one tradition that will never fade away: Christmas movies. Those endlessly rewatchable visual snow globes of nostalgia remind us why we try our best every year to create memories for others.

Before you embark on this journey through the most magical of film genres, think long and hard about what you think defines a Christmas movie. The inclusion of *Die Hard* in the Christmas movie canon is the granddaddy of argument gasoline. Some people say it's a Christmas movie, some people say it's not a Christmas movie, and some say it's *the* Christmas movie.

Ultimately, all that matters is what you think, and what movies you love. I hope you appreciate my painstaking research to include enough titles on the list to make it worthy of the word "ultimate." Now, it's time to flip through these pages and learn a thing or two as you pass the seven levels of the candy-cane forest, ring a bell, shoot your eye out, and celebrate the most magical time of the year.

This book is my gift to you. I hope you honor Christmas in your heart and try to keep it all year long. Just do me one favor: don't become a Scrooge. Otherwise, well, you know the rest . . .

BAH HUMBUG

How to Use This Book

Within these pages, you'll find a collection (that we checked at least twice) of quizzes and references to more than one hundred of the best Christmas movies of all time.

That's right. Every quiz was tailor-made to each film, and unless you're a Bad Santa and don't care for rules, we highly recommend you watch or rewatch the movies before diving in to play.

Now spring into action and grab onto the sleigh, get ready for questions to score right away, we hope that this new book will make your season bright, "Merry Quiz-Mas to all, and to all a good night!"

Visual Cheer-O-Meter

To help you on your Christmas journey, we've consulted the world's foremost authorities on Christmas movies (because all the scientists were apparently "busy") and asked one hundred people to rate the marquee films (on a scale from 1 to 5) in the following categories:

Christmas Spirit

Music, Decorations, Holiday Vibes, Holiday Tenets, Message

Warm Fuzzies

Feel Goodness, Coziness, Romance, Heartwarmer, Happy Ending

Timelessness

Quotability, Importance, Rewatchability, Classic Status, Accessibility

The Twelve Chapters of Christmas

The main quizzes of the book are where you'll find eight gift-wrapped, multiple-choice questions on a particular film in a specific Christmas subgenre. Questions are worth 1 point apiece for a total of 8 possible points per quiz. Total possible points: 480

Spotlight Quiz

Five multiple choice questions on a special film (or films) that couldn't quite earn a spot in the top five movies of each chapter but is included for its importance to the subgenre, the film history, or Christmas movies in general. Questions are worth 1 point apiece for a total of 5 possible points per quiz. Total possible points: 30

Jingle Bell Bonus

Fun bite-sized, matching quizzes that include underrated, underseen, or underappreciated films within a chapter's subgenre. Earn 1 point for each question, for a total of 5 points per quiz. Total possible points: 55.

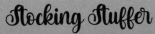

Stocking Stuffer

You've spent all day struggling to assemble that dollhouse, kitchen play set, and bicycle. It's time to take a break from trying to ace those five eight-question quizzes and take a palate-cleanser. Expect a single quiz of ten questions (with no multiple choice) from a particular type of Christmas movie that didn't get a full chapter. For your troubles, earn 1 point per question. Total possible points: 40

Keep Score

Keep track of scores for yourself or your friends. There are 605 points up for grabs if you play through this entire book! Tabulate your scores and see where you rank:

Final Score: _____

1-201 Points
Christmas Curmudgeon

It may have started off rough, but by the end, you found redemption and fully embraced the spirit of Christmas. Like Ebenezer Scrooge and the Grinch, you let Christmas into your heart, and it even grew a few sizes.

202-402 Points
Santa's Little Helper

You are Santa's secret weapon for saving Christmas. You join the ranks of Buddy the Elf, Cindy Lou Who, and Rudolph the Red-Nosed Reindeer, making sure that everyone wakes up happy on Christmas morning.

403-605 Points
The Christmas Star

Like the most important element of a Christmas tree, you are the shining example of Christmas spirit and follow in the footsteps of Christmas legends like George Bailey, Kevin McCallister, and Clark Griswold. Bravo!

Bah, Humbug!

ADAPTATIONS OF
A CHRISTMAS CAROL

It's not really Christmas unless you watch *A Christmas Carol*. It's as simple as that. And that's not just a bit of undigested beef talking; that's a fact as cold as the piercing, searching, biting freeze of a Victorian winter. The tale of Ebenezer Scrooge, a penny-pinching miser whose frigid heart is warmed by ghostly visitors who show him the error of his ways, redefined the holiday season. When the novella was released in 1843, Britain was exploring and reevaluating traditions of Christmases past—like singing carols—while adopting new traditions like sending cards and decorating Christmas trees. Nearly two hundred years later, this story is *the* holiday staple. From Michael Caine to Mickey Mouse, Murray to Muppets, what makes all the adaptations of *A Christmas Carol* so much fun is that the character of Scrooge is endlessly ripe for reinvention. The story is always the same, but each version finds a new way of highlighting its themes: compassion, redemption, generosity, and embracing the true spirit of Christmas.

A Christmas Carol

Cheer-O-Meter

Christmas Spirit

Warm Fuzzies

Timelessness

Year: 2009

Director: Robert Zemeckis

Writer: Robert Zemeckis

Cast: Jim Carrey, Gary Oldman, Colin Firth, Bob Hoskins, Robin Wright

Plot: From the team behind *The Polar Express* comes a vividly reimagined take on Charles Dickens's classic using groundbreaking motion-capture technology.

1. Before the opening title card, Scrooge is at the undertaker's to sign the death certificate of his business partner, Jacob Marley. What adjustment does Scrooge make to the corpse to the surprise of the undertaker's young apprentice?

   A. He takes the coins off Marley's eyes

   B. He fastens Marley's chin strap

   C. He fixes Marley's tie

   D. He takes Marley's silver brooch

2. After finding out he's getting Christmas Day off work, Bob Cratchit runs into the streets and partakes in what activity "in honor of Christmas Eve"?

   A. A snowball fight

   B. Making snowmen

   C. Singing carols

   D. Sliding on ice down the hilly street

3. **The Ghost of Christmas Past is portrayed a bit differently in this film than in other adaptations with what object clearly the inspiration behind its look and feel?**

   A. He looks like an angel

   B. He looks like a candle

   C. He looks like a book

   D. He looks like a poinsettia

4. **During Fezziwig's party, the fiddler providing the music has what unexpected finale that results in raucous applause from the attendees?**

   A. He accidentally knocks over the Christmas tree

   B. He accidentally breaks all his strings

   C. He accidentally falls into a bowl of punch

   D. He accidentally lights himself on fire

5. **When Scrooge encounters the Ghost of Christmas Present in a room filled with golden clocks and Christmas decorations, he asks the Ghost if he has many brothers. How many brothers does the Ghost say he has?**

   A. 1,842

   B. 1,852

   C. 1,862

   D. 1,882

BAH HUMBUG

6. When Scrooge sees his own tombstone and begins to repent to the Ghost of Christmas Yet to Come, in what way does he transition back to reality the next morning?

   A. He collapses on the snow and wakes up in his bedsheets

   B. He is put in a snow vortex and flown in the air and lands on his bedroom carpet

   C. He falls into his own grave and awakes hanging upside down by the curtains above his bed

   D. The ghost hearse runs over him, and he wakes up in his chair next to the fireplace

7. A reformed Scrooge walks through the streets on Christmas morning wishing good tidings to people around him and joining carolers singing what Christmas carol?

   A. "Joy to the World"

   B. "God Rest Ye Merry, Gentlemen"

   C. "Deck the Halls"

   D. "We Wish You a Merry Christmas"

8. During the finale, what character breaks the fourth wall and recites text from the book *A Christmas Carol* to end the story?

   A. Scrooge

   B. Tiny Tim

   C. Bob Cratchit

   D. Fred

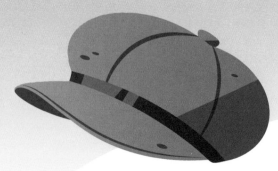

ANSWERS: 1.A, 2.D, 3.B, 4.C, 5.A, 6.C, 7.A, 8.C

Scrooge

Year: 1951 (Released in the United States as *A Christmas Carol*)

Director: Brian Desmond Hurst

Writer: Noel Langley

Cast: Alastair Sim, Jack Warner, Kathleen Harrison, Mervyn Johns, Hermione Baddeley

Plot: Many consider this to be the definitive live-action version of the Dickens novella. The film's atmospheric black-and-white cinematography and compelling performance by Scottish character actor Alastair Sim tell a somber version of Scrooge's tale.

Cheer-O-Meter

Christmas Spirit

Warm Fuzzies

Timelessness

1. On his way to work (where he disparages two men collecting for the poor), Scrooge barks at three children for singing which Christmas carol?

    A. "O Holy Night"

    B. "Silent Night"

    C. "The First Noel"

    D. "Coventry Carol"

2. The first time we see Tiny Tim on-screen is outside in the cold, doing what with a big smile on his face?

   A. Making a snowman

   B. Having a snowball fight with his brother Peter

   C. Walking hand in hand with his mother over a footbridge

   D. Gazing through a toy-shop window

3. Bob Cratchit wishes Scrooge a merry Christmas, but Scrooge balks, incredulous that a clerk with a family could have a merry Christmas making how much money a week?

   A. 15 shillings

   B. 12 shillings

   C. 10 shillings

   D. 4 shillings

4. When Scrooge is alone in his vast, dark home on Christmas Eve, mere minutes before the ghost of his former business partner and friend, Jacob Marley, arrives, he eats what food?

   A. A bit of beef

   B. A stack of dry crackers

   C. A bowl of gruel

   D. An underdone potato

Festive Fact

When Scrooge wakes up, grateful to be alive, he makes his way to a mirror by the window twice. On both occasions, if you look very closely at the bottom left-hand corner of the mirror, you'll see a crew member.

5. This version of Dickens's classic takes some liberties with the original story by creating a plotline suggesting Scrooge resents his nephew, Fred, for what reason?

   A. Fred loves Christmas

   B. Fred doesn't respect his mother's memory

   C. Fred never accepted his offer to work for him

   D. Scrooge's sister, Fan, died while giving birth to Fred

6. Another liberty taken from the novel is a name change for Belle, Scrooge's past fiancée and the love of his life. Here, Belle goes by what name?

   A. Alice

   B. Bella

   C. Ella

   D. Lily

7. Before the Ghost of Christmas Present departs, he gives one final warning to Scrooge by showing him two emaciated children under his robe. He says the children represent what?

   A. The boy is neglect, the girl is desire

   B. The boy is want, the girl is ignorance

   C. The boy is ignorance, the girl is want

   D. The boy is innocence, the girl is hope

8. On Christmas Day, Scrooge realizes he's still alive and rejoices with Mrs. Dilber, who is shocked at his enthusiasm. While jumping up and down, Scrooge says he feels like all but which of these?

   A. As mad as a hatter

   B. As light as a feather

   C. As happy as an angel

   D. As giddy as a drunken man

ANSWERS: 1.B, 2.D, 3.A, 4.C, 5.D, 6.A, 7.C, 8.A

Scrooged

Year: 1988

Director: Richard Donner

Writers: Mitch Glazer, Michael O'Donoghue

Cast: Bill Murray, Karen Allen, John Forsythe, John Glover, Bobcat Goldthwait

Plot: This modern retelling of *A Christmas Carol* follows cynical and selfish TV executive Frank Cross who is encouraged by a series of ghosts to reevaluate his actions and to right the wrongs of his past.

Cheer-O-Meter

Christmas Spirit

Warm Fuzzies

Timelessness

1. **The film opens with what turns out to be a series of ads for the IBC network containing all but which of the following television programs or specials?**

    A. *Mrs. Claus Goes Malibu*

    B. Bob Goulet's *Old Fashioned Cajun Christmas*

    C. *Father Loves Beaver*

    D. *The Night the Reindeer Died*

TAXI FARE

2. **In this modern retelling, the Ghost of Christmas Past is portrayed in what unique way compared to other versions?**

A. A zombified golfer

B. A wisecracking taxi driver

C. An unpredictably violent fairy

D. A sardonic fireman

3. **Frank Cross is overseeing IBC's biggest event, a live broadcast of *A Christmas Carol*, which features all but which of these celebrity cameos in notable roles?**

A. Olympian Mary Lou Retton as Tiny Tim

B. Jamie Farr as Jacob Marley

C. Kareem Abdul-Jabbar as the Ghost of Christmas Yet to Come

D. Buddy Hackett as Scrooge

4. **Frank, age four, asks his father for a choo-choo train for Christmas, but much to the dismay of his pregnant mother, he receives what gift because "life doesn't come on a silver platter"?**

A. A sheet of aluminum siding

B. Five pounds of veal

C. A rusted set of silverware

D. A monogrammed towel

Festive Fact

During the final monologue, Frank Cross says, "Feed me, Seymour!"—a direct reference to the movie and musical *Little Shop of Horrors*.

5. With the Ghost of Christmas Past, Frank rewatches his relationship with Claire crash and burn. Claire's last image of Frank is him performing as what canine TV character?

A. Frisbee

B. Sparky

C. Buzz

D. Corduroy

6. Claire reappears in Frank's life after he calls her in terror following a visit from his long-dead mentor, Lew Hayward. Claire has been working as the director of what shelter for the homeless?

A. Operation Give Back

B. Operation Open Heart

C. Operation Reach Out

D. Operation Stay Warm

7. In a bit of trivia inside trivia, the Ghost of Christmas Present takes Frank to a party thrown by his brother, James, and James's wife, where he sees them unable to answer what specific question?

A. What is the name of the luxury cruise liner on *The Love Boat*?

B. What is the name of the trusty car on *Knight Rider*?

C. What is the name of the handler on *Charlie's Angels*?

D. What is the name of the boat that took everyone to Gilligan's Island?

8. The Ghost of Christmas Future doesn't show Frank his tombstone in a cemetery like most adaptations and instead takes him on a special elevator ride to show him what?

A. His funeral

B. His own cremation

C. His body flatlining at the hospital

D. What his life is like in hell

Spirited

Year: 2022

Director: Sean Anders

Writers: Sean Anders, John Morris

Cast: Will Ferrell, Ryan Reynolds, Octavia Spencer, Sunita Mani, Patrick Page

Plot: On Christmas Eve, the Ghost of Christmas Present faces an unexpected challenge when he selects Clint Briggs for a transformative Christmas haunting.

Cheer-O-Meter

Christmas Spirit

Warm Fuzzies

Timelessness

1. Described as "the perfect combination of Mussolini and Seacrest," Clint Briggs is first shown conning what festive convention into preserving the American way of life?

    A. National Association of Christmas Tree Growers

    B. National Association of Independent Toy Makers

    C. National Association of Christmas Light Displays

    D. National Association of Christmas Wreath Makers

2. Clint assigns his longtime assistant, Kimberly, to do oppo research for his niece, Wren, on her opponent for class president, Joshua. Kimberly finds what damning evidence that has her riddled with guilt?

    A. Joshua knocking over the town's Christmas tree

    B. Joshua egging the principal's house

    C. Joshua at a homeless shelter calling it gross

    D. Joshua stealing donated presents

3. During his heavily orchestrated haunt, Clint remarks on the astounding level of detail except for what popular retail chain that didn't exist in his past?

A. Sephora

B. Bed Bath & Beyond

C. Bath & Body Works

D. Urban Outfitters

4. Clint is shown a memory from when he visited his dying sister, Carrie, and declined her request to take care of her daughter, Wren. What word does the Spirit Crew use for this key moment from someone's past that must be faced to affect real change?

A. Gut punch

B. Clincher

C. Kicker

D. Haymaker

5. In a major twist to the story, Present goes off-script and uses an unconventional approach to get through to Clint, taking him back to his own past and revealing that he is what fellow unredeemable?

A. Oliver Cromwell

B. Edwin Drood

C. John Elwes

D. Ebenezer Scrooge

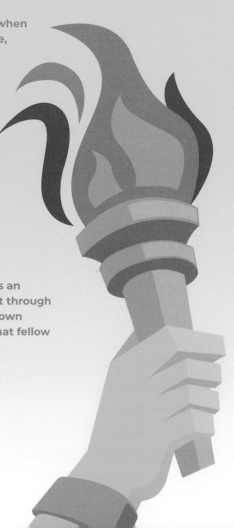

6. What two-word phrase effectively means "f you!" in the Spirited universe and is also the title of a show-stopping number by Clint as he attempts to cheer up Present?

    A. Good Day

    B. Good Evening

    C. Good Afternoon

    D. Good Riddance

7. The aforementioned song features a lyric about what Oscar-winning actress who makes a surprise cameo in the film as a villager walking by the action?

    A. Helen Mirren

    B. Judi Dench

    C. Maggie Smith

    D. Olivia Colman

8. Which one of the futures are NOT shown during the epilogue and reprise?

    A. Clint is now Ghost of Christmas Present, dating Past, and working with Carrie

    B. Present is happily married to Kimberly, and they have two kids together

    C. The operation has added Ghosts of Ramadan Past and Hanukkah Yet to Come

    D. Jacob Marley has retired and is a singing bartender on a cruise ship

The Muppet Christmas Carol

Year: 1992

Director: Brian Henson

Writer: Jerry Juhl

Cast: Michael Caine, Dave Goelz, Steve Whitmire, Jerry Nelson, Frank Oz

Plot: This festive perennial infuses Dickens's story with whimsical Muppet charm.

Cheer-O-Meter

Christmas Spirit

Warm Fuzzies

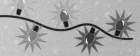

Timelessness

1. This adaptation includes Charles Dickens as narrator. He is played by what Muppet?

   A. Kermit

   B. Sam the Eagle

   C. Rowlf the Dog

   D. Gonzo

2. Joining Charles Dickens as his sidekick is Rizzo the Rat. He's also the only Muppet in the film to have what distinction?

   A. The only Muppet who says the first and last word of the film

   B. The only Muppet who doesn't sing

   C. The only Muppet to be credited "As Himself" during the opening titles

   D. The only Muppet to be involved with a CGI shot

3. In this adaptation, Jacob Marley became two brothers, Jacob and Robert Marley, portrayed by what Muppets?

   A. Waldorf and Statler

   B. Bert and Ernie

   C. Bunsen and Beaker

   D. Biff and Sully

4. The character of Fezziwig, or "Fozziwig," played to perfection by none other than Fozzie Bear, is Scrooge's first employer and the owner of a factory that specialized in what goods?

   A. Neckties

   B. Top hats

   C. Rubber chickens

   D. Decorative wigs

5. During Fozziwig's Christmas party, where Scrooge meets Belle, the Swedish Chef is shown serving what delicacy?

   A. Onions

   B. Grapes

   C. Cabbage

   D. Tomatoes

6. As the Ghost of Christmas Past shows Scrooge his old schoolroom aging and decaying, Dickens and Rizzo sit on a shelf containing all but which of the following marble busts?

   A. Shakespeare

   B. Aristotle

   C. Dante

   D. Galileo

7. Emily Cratchit addresses the dinner table and reluctantly gives a toast in honor of Scrooge and does NOT use which of the following descriptors?

   A. Odious

   B. Wicked

   C. Miserly

   D. Badly dressed

8. Can you complete Rizzo's quote before he became acquainted with a bucket of freezing water? "Light the ____, not the ____!"

   A. Candle, handle

   B. Stove, apron

   C. Lamp, rat

   D. Lantern, cheese

ANSWERS: 1.D, 2.C, 3.A, 4.C, 5.B, 6.D, 7.C, 8.C

Match the Miser to the Movie

With over one hundred adaptations of *A Christmas Carol*, there's no shortage of renowned actors who have played one of the most famous roles in history. Can you match the miser (actor playing Scrooge) to the movie in which he appears?

1. *A Christmas Carol* (1999)

2. *Mickey's Christmas Carol* (1983)

3. *The Man Who Invented Christmas* (2017)

4. *Scrooge* (1970)

5. *A Christmas Carol* (1984)

A. George C. Scott

B. Christopher Plummer

C. Patrick Stewart

D. Scrooge McDuck

E. Albert Finney

POST-CREDITS

★ The group of starving musicians playing a cover of "We Three Kings" that Frank Cross belittles at the beginning of *Scrooged* weren't just any street musicians. The ensemble was made up of guitarist Larry Carlton, saxophonist David Sanborn, legendary *Late Show* bandleader Paul Shaffer, and jazz legend Miles Davis on trumpet.

★ *The Muppet Christmas Carol* was the first Muppet movie made without their creator, Jim Henson, who had passed away just two years before it was made. Henson's son, Brian, carried on his legacy by making this revered classic his directorial debut.

★ *Disney's A Christmas Carol* utilized performance-capture technology that allowed actors to play multiple parts and be reimagined in post-production. Jim Carrey played eight characters (Ebenezer Scrooge at various ages and all three ghosts) and Gary Oldman played three (Jacob Marley, Bob Cratchit, and Tiny Tim).

BAH, HUMBUG!

Dashing through the Stunts

ACTION, ADVENTURE, AND CRIME

*C*ue voiceover legend Don LaFontaine: "In a world where Christmas movies are synonymous with sugar-coated sentimentality, a beloved subgenre rises from the ashes. It dares to create a holly-jolly and high-octane holiday tradition that replaces tinsel with TNT and swaps the cozy flicker of a fireplace with the fiery glow of a well-timed (and slow-motion escaped) explosion."

This is Christmas at its most thrilling—a time for heroes and antiheroes to save their beloved city, rescue a failed marriage, or watch as the real Santa Claus liberates a family from a group of mercenaries who barked up the wrong chimney. This catalog of Christmas-themed celluloid wish fulfillment comprises instantly rewatchable flicks that provide escapism and deliver a gift basket chock-full of ammo, iconic characters, clever quips, and visual spectacles.

Many of these films are the subject of heated debates regarding their place in the Christmas canon, but while all points are valid, the Internet tells us that the Christmas season doesn't begin until Hans Gruber falls from Nakatomi Plaza. Ho-Ho-Ho.

Batman Returns

Year: 1992

Director: Tim Burton

Writer: Daniel Waters (story by Daniel Waters and Sam Hamm)

Cast: Michael Keaton, Danny DeVito, Michelle Pfeiffer, Christopher Walken, Michael Gough

Plot: In this chilling sequel to 1989's *Batman*, the caped crusader faces a dual threat in snowy Gotham City: a power-hungry Penguin taking on the city's elite and a whip-wielding Catwoman out for personal vengeance.

Cheer-O-Meter

Christmas Spirit

Warm Fuzzies

Timelessness

1. **Tucker and Esther Cobblepot abandon their infant son, Oswald (a.k.a. Penguin), in the sewers. He is adopted by a family of penguins and sets up his lair in what Gotham Zoo exhibit?**

   A. Arctic Adventure

   B. Arctic World

   C. Arctic Encounter

   D. Arctic Frontier

2. After being pushed out a window by Max Schreck, Selina Kyle breaks letters on a neon sign that creates what two-word phrase?

   A. Hell Here

   B. Hell Below

   C. Hell Now

   D. Hell Ahead

3. Catwoman straddles Batman on a moonlit rooftop and tells him that, "If you mean it . . . a kiss can be even deadlier" than what?

   A. Whips

   B. Guns

   C. Bombs

   D. Mistletoe

4. Mayor Murphy hopes that Gotham will have its first merry Christmas in years. But that hope is destroyed at the tree-lighting ceremony when Max Schreck is kidnapped. What is the name of the barbaric circus gang that kidnaps him?

   A. The Red Diamond Gang

   B. The Red Triangle Gang

   C. The Red Skull Gang

   D. The Red Dragon Gang

5. The Penguin's favorite form of transportation is an all-terrain vehicle. What animal was this vehicle fashioned after?

   A. Swan

   B. Crane

   C. Duck

   D. Turtle

6. **In Bruce's study, where is the secret switch located that, when pressed, opens a chute inside an iron maiden leading directly into the Batcave?**

   A.   A model of Wayne Manor in a fish tank

   B.   A bust of Shakespeare

   C.   A book on the bookshelf

   D.   Under the desk

7. **Catwoman says that Schreck killed her, Batman killed her, and Penguin killed her, which means three of her nine lives are gone. After her confrontation with Schreck ends with an electric kiss, how many lives are left?**

   A.   Three

   B.   Two

   C.   One

   D.   Zero

8. **The film ends with Bruce finding a stray cat in a snowy alley before he and Alfred drive off into the Tim Burton version of a sunset, with Bruce saying:**

   A.   "Merry Christmas, Gotham."

   B.   "Goodwill toward men. And women."

   C.   "Back to the house, Alfred."

   D.   "A bat, with a cat. Who would have thought."

Festive Fact

Savvy sneakerheads know that if you want to dress like Michael Keaton's Batman, you don't need boots or billions of dollars. The Batsuit in *Batman Returns* features Air Jordan VI sneakers with some extra padding.

Die Hard

Cheer-O-Meter

Christmas Spirit

Warm Fuzzies

Timelessness

Year: 1988

Director: John McTiernan

Writers: Jeb Stuart, Steven E. de Souza

Cast: Bruce Willis, Alan Rickman, Bonnie Bedelia, Reginald VelJohnson, Alexander Godunov

Plot: NYPD Detective John McClane journeys to Los Angeles on Christmas Eve to reunite with his estranged wife. But when a group of ruthless terrorists seize control of Nakatomi Plaza, McClane is thrust into a high-stakes game.

1. **McClane is picked up by first-time limo driver Argyle, a charismatic driver who serves as an ally to him throughout the film. As they arrive at Nakatomi Plaza, what song does Argyle play on the tape deck?**

   A. "Santa's Rap" by Treacherous Three

   B. "Christmas Rappin'" by Kurtis Blow

   C. "Christmas in Hollis" by Run-D.M.C.

   D. "Chillin' With Santa" by Derek B

2. Hans Gruber is at Nakatomi Plaza to retrieve what specific loot inside the vault with seven safeguards?

   A. $640 million in cash

   B. $640 million in negotiable bearer bonds

   C. $640 million in gold bullion

   D. $640 million in Deutsche Mark

3. What taunting phrase did McClane write on Tony's sweater before sending his Santa-hat-wearing corpse down an elevator to Hans?

   A. Now I have a machine gun. Ho-Ho-Ho.

   B. Now I have a rifle. Ho-Ho-Ho.

   C. Now I have the detonators. Ho-Ho-Ho.

   D. Now I have the upper hand. Ho-Ho-Ho.

4. McClane has a verbal joust with Hans, who says McClane is just another American who saw too many movies as a child. After Hans lists off potential cinematic heroes, McClane says he is partial to whom?

   A. Rambo

   B. John Wayne

   C. Roy Rogers

   D. Marshal Dillon

Festive Fact

The scene of John McClane falling in the ventilation shaft and slipping past an opening only to catch himself was unplanned. A stuntman fell past his catch point and the editor decided to incorporate the fall into the final edit.

5. Sergeant Al Powell of the LAPD is a lot of things: a self-confessed desk jockey, traumatized after wrongfully firing his weapon; in a walkie-talkie bromance with McClane; and weak for what sweet treat?

   A. Donuts

   B. Twinkies

   C. Ding Dongs

   D. Ho Hos

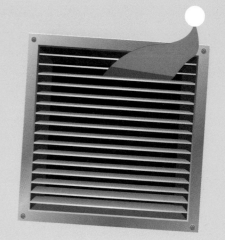

6. What is the name of the slimy exec who "negotiate[s] million-dollar deals for breakfast" and puts the safety of McClane and the hostages in danger thanks to his own hubris?

   A. Elton

   B. Ellison

   C. Elwin

   D. Ellis

7. Uli, a henchman with a sweet tooth, steals what candy bar before a shootout with the LAPD SWAT team?

   A. Hershey's

   B. Baby Ruth

   C. Crunch

   D. Snickers

8. Every cinematic bad guy needs good bad-guy music. Hans Gruber has composer Michael Kamen weaving in the timeless Beethoven choral piece from Symphony no. 9, more commonly referred to as what?

   A. "Ode to Joy"

   B. "Joy to the World"

   C. "Joyful Joyful"

   D. "Messiah"

Reindeer Games

Year: 2000

Director: John Frankenheimer

Writer: Ehren Kruger

Cast: Ben Affleck, Gary Sinise, Charlize Theron, Dennis Farina, James Frain

Plot: Recently released convict Rudy Duncan assumes the identity of his cellmate, Nick, to be with Nick's pen-pal girlfriend, Ashley, for the holidays. But plans go awry when Rudy is coerced to rob a casino on Christmas Eve.

Cheer-O-Meter

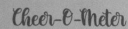

Christmas Spirit

Warm Fuzzies

Timelessness

1. In the lead-up to Christmas, Rudy and his best friend, Nick, are days from release at Iron Mountain State Prison. Rudy tells Nick that the first thing he's gonna have when he gets out is what?

   A. Cookies

   B. Dad's Christmas turkey

   C. Holiday Jell-O

   D. Hot chocolate

Festive Fact

Oscar winner Isaac Hayes makes a cameo as an inmate named Zook. He received a standing ovation from extras after his scene was filmed.

2. **Rudy and Ashley are kidnapped by a gang of toughs run by Ashley's criminal brother, who goes by what nickname?**

   A. Nighthawk

   B. Beast

   C. Monster

   D. Gabriel

3. **Jumpy (played by Danny Trejo) is a business-minded criminal who proposes legislating a second gift-giving holiday in May or June to stimulate growth with what name?**

   A. May Giving

   B. Christmas Two

   C. June-mas

   D. Spring-a-thon

4. **Rudy is pressed over pecan pie to provide details on the Tomahawk Casino, where Nick used to work security. The only piece of information keeping him alive is that he mentions a special safe in the manager's office that goes by what name?**

   A. Shangri-la

   B. The treasure box

   C. The gold chest

   D. The pow-wow safe

5. **Jack Bangs, the casino head who can't go back to Vegas, runs a business with staff that shows 16 percent more skin than competitors and has what special amenity?**

   A. Saunas in the bathroom

   B. A buffet that serves both Coke and Pepsi

   C. Free steak Saturdays

   D. Fantasy fulfillment center

6. In a blink-and-you'll-miss-it cameo, what TV/film actor appears as a college student who switches clothes with Rudy (in a cowboy disguise) and gets chased down by thugs?

   A. Ashton Kutcher

   B. John Krasinski

   C. Aaron Paul

   D. Jason Segel

7. Rudy and the rest of the gang all wear what kind of outfit for the big casino heist that goes off the rails thanks to Rudy's incorrect instructions?

   A. Jumpsuits and ski masks

   B. Cowboy outfits

   C. Santa Claus outfits

   D. Security guard uniforms

8. What is Rudy's favorite Christmas song, which he hums throughout the film? It's played during the epilogue when, dressed as Santa, Rudy puts stacks of cash in strangers' mailboxes.

   A. "Here Comes Santa Claus"

   B. "Santa Claus Is Coming to Town"

   C. "Feliz Navidad"

   D. "The Little Drummer Boy"

ANSWERS: 1. D, 2. C, 3. B, 4. D, 5. B, 6. A, 7. C, 8. D

The Ref

Year: 1994

Director: Ted Demme

Writers: Richard LaGravenese, Marie Weiss

Cast: Denis Leary, Judy Davis, Kevin Spacey, Glynis Johns, Raymond J. Barry

Plot: Attempting to lie low from the authorities after a botched robbery on Christmas Eve, cat burglar Gus finds himself an unwilling marital referee to the relentless bickering of the feuding married couple he holds hostage.

Cheer-O-Meter

Christmas Spirit

Warm Fuzzies

Timelessness

1. On Christmas Eve, Lloyd and Caroline are in the midst of a counseling session. The discussion ranges from an affair to Lloyd's overbearing mother and a dream about a head on a platter. What is the name of their marriage counselor?

    A. Dr. Wong

    B. Dr. Watson

    C. Dr. Lee

    D. Dr. Morin

2. Where does Gus find Murray—his loser of a partner—when he calls him from the Chausseurs' phone looking for an escape plan?

A. The Seventeenth Hole

B. The Mackerel Lounge

C. Brixie's Pub

D. Doc Ryan's

Festive Fact

The movie originally had a different ending. Gus was going to sacrifice himself in some way to help the family, but Disney stepped in and wanted a happy ending.

3. In order to control Caroline and Lloyd, Gus needs to tie them up. They don't have any rope in the house, so what does Gus use to keep them from running away?

A. Tinsel

B. Duct tape

C. Extension cords

D. Bungee cords

4. The Santa Claus in this film, a lush named George, has a bone to pick with everyone who doesn't reciprocate his gift giving. George doesn't have a Naughty or Nice List but instead, what kind of list?

A. Fruitcake list

B. Sausage list

C. Steak list

D. Wine list

5. Gus notices an original work of art in Caroline and Lloyd's house. The artwork makes Caroline angry because it reminds her of her mother-in-law, but it makes Gus angry because they don't appreciate it. Who is the artist?

A. Hopper

B. Chagall

C. Rockwell

D. Mondrian

6. The inept and inexperienced officers of Old Baybrook find themselves with nothing to do, so they watch what holiday movie on TV?

   A. *National Lampoon's Christmas Vacation*

   B. *White Christmas*

   C. *The Bishop's Wife*

   D. *It's a Wonderful Life*

7. Caroline prepares a traditional Scandinavian feast for Christmas dinner that includes roast suckling pig and seven-day-old lutefisk. She even makes everyone wear candles on their heads in honor of what saint?

   A. Lorens

   B. Lucille

   C. Lucia

   D. Larsson

8. Caroline and Lloyd bare their souls in front of their family and Lloyd finally stands up to his mother, Rose. Lloyd's sister-in-law, Connie, decides to stand up for herself too. How does she answer Rose's accusation, "Who the hell do you think you are?"

   A. "Slipper socks. Small."

   B. "Slipper socks. Medium."

   C. "Slipper socks. Large."

   D. "Slipper socks. Adjustable."

Festive Fact

Star of stage and screen Glynis Johns plays the role of Lloyd's overbearing mother, Rose. You may remember her as Winifred, the matriarch of the Banks family in *Mary Poppins.*

Violent Night

Year: 2022

Director: Tommy Wirkola

Writers: Pat Casey, Josh Miller

Cast: David Harbour, John Leguizamo, Alex Hassell, Alexis Louder, Beverly D'Angelo

Plot: When a group of mercenaries invades an estate on Christmas Eve, all that stands between them and millions of dollars is a jaded Santa Claus.

Cheer-O-Meter

Christmas Spirit

Warm Fuzzies

Timelessness

1. The film opens in a bar with a salty Santa Claus considering retirement. Before he leaves, what gift does Santa give the bartender?

    A. Two tickets to a Knicks game

    B. A new puppy

    C. The bike she wanted as a child

    D. A video game for her grandson

2. A group of mercenaries led by Mr. Scrooge raids the G. T. Lightstone family compound and quickly disposes of its private security. All the henchmen grudgingly use festive code names, including all but which of the following?

    A. Rudolph

    B. Krampus

    C. Sugarplum

    D. Candy Cane

Festive Fact

The song "Christmas Time" by Bryan Adams is featured prominently in the film thanks to director Tommy Wirkola, who remembered it playing constantly during the holidays in his native Norway.

3. Gertrude is played by Beverly D'Angelo, the same actress who famously played another family matriarch in which Christmas movie?

A. *The Santa Clause*

B. *A Christmas Story*

C. *National Lampoon's Christmas Vacation*

D. *Jingle All the Way*

4. Jason feels guilty for not taking his daughter, Trudy, to see Santa and gives her what early makeshift Christmas gift that comes in handy?

A. A flare gun

B. A cell phone

C. An iPad

D. A walkie-talkie

5. While nursing his wounds, Santa speaks with Trudy about his origins. He reveals he was a Viking whose weapon of choice was a hammer called what?

A. Skullcrusher

B. Bonecrusher

C. Stormbreaker

D. Leviathan

6. What film does Trudy watch for the first time the night before Christmas Eve that serves as inspiration for her when trying to survive the onslaught of henchmen in the family home?

A. *Raiders of the Lost Ark*

B. *The Goonies*

C. *Home Alone*

D. *John Wick*

7. The boyfriend of Gertrude's daughter, Alva, is a wannabe Jean-Claude Van Damme, who is kind of a big deal in Asia. The boyfriend is the first hostage to escape and the first hostage to see the end credits early. What is his name?

A. John Matrix

B. Darren McCord

C. Lincoln Hawk

D. Morgan Steel

8. When Scrooge and Commander Thorp discover that the family vault is empty, it's revealed that "Mom's favorite" Jason stole the money to get out of his mother's shadow and start a new life. Where did he hide the money?

A. Inside the tool shed

B. Inside the Nativity scene

C. Inside the attic

D. Inside the Christmas tree

Shane Black and the Christmas Backdrop

When Shane Black kicked Hollywood's door down with his script for *Lethal Weapon*, he not only became one of the most in-demand screenwriters of all time, he rewrote the blueprint of the modern action movie. His style is like a batch of cinematic Christmas cookies: one part witty banter, two parts intricate plotting, and a handful of flawed but relatable characters. Put it all together and you have a shoot-'em-up movie unlike anything seen before and repeatedly copied since.

But Black's secret sauce isn't just the magic that comes from his keyboard . . . it's Christmas. His trademark of setting films during the holidays offers a stark contrast between the warmth of Christmas and the violence his films often portray.

1. *Lethal Weapon*, the first film in the Shane Black oeuvre to have Christmas as a backdrop, starts with a bang by featuring what Christmas song over the opening credits?

    A. "Christmas (Baby Please Come Home)" by Darlene Love

    B. "Rockin' around the Christmas Tree" by Brenda Lee

    C. "Jingle Bell Rock" by Bobby Helms

    D. "Run Rudolph Run" by Chuck Berry

2. In *Kiss Kiss Bang Bang*, Harry Lockhart is a small-time criminal trying to rob a toy store for a cyber agent figure for Christmas. To avoid the authorities, where does Harry accidentally end up going?

    A. A holiday work party

    B. A Hollywood audition

    C. A tree-lighting ceremony

    D. An ice-sculpture contest

3. While the film has one of the thinnest elements of Christmas for a Shane Black movie, *The Nice Guys* does end on a high note. After successfully closing their case, Healy and March celebrate their new detective agency at a Christmas-decorated restaurant of what food variety?

   A. Mexican

   B. Ethiopian

   C. Thai

   D. Chinese

4. Shane Black took over directing the *Iron Man* franchise from Jon Favreau with *Iron Man 3*. The film has several references to Christmas, including one scene where Tony gets Pepper what oversized Christmas present?

   A. Giant stuffed teddy bear

   B. Giant stuffed puppy

   C. Giant stuffed penguin

   D. Giant stuffed octopus

5. Geena Davis plays the dual role of caring single mother and deadly assassin in *The Long Kiss Goodnight*. She is dressed up as what holiday character in the Christmas parade at the beginning of the film?

   A. Cindy Lou Who

   B. Mary, from the Nativity

   C. Rudolph the Red-Nosed Reindeer

   D. Mrs. Claus

ANSWERS: 1.C, 2.B, 3.A, 4.B, 5.D

JINGLE BELL BONUS

Elflix and Chill

Sometimes on a cold, wintry night, the best medicine for the Christmas blues is watching things blow up, heroes defeat villains, and the Christmas spirit being taught through knuckle sandwiches. Can you match the cell phones with emoji movie recommendations with the film?

1.

2.

3.

4.

5.

A. *The Ice Harvest* (2005)

B. *Invasion U.S.A.* (1985)

C. *Trapped in Paradise* (1994)

D. *Silent Night* (2023)

E. *The Silent Partner* (1978)

POST-CREDITS

⭐ Marlon Wayans was cast to play Robin in **Batman Returns** and a proposed third sequel, but the character was ultimately cut from the script. Then, when director Joel Schumacher took over the franchise, he had a different vision and hired Chris O'Donnell. Thankfully, Wayans was paid for his time and still receives residuals for the Bat sequel.

⭐ Future Oscar-winning actor J. K. Simmons (*Whiplash*) made his big-screen debut in **The Ref** as Colonel Siskel, the military-school commanding officer who Jesse is blackmailing. Screenwriter/producer Richard LaGravenese named the character of Siskel after Gene Siskel as revenge for comments the noted film critic made about an earlier script of his.

⭐ **Violent Night** references a ton of holiday classics, like *Die Hard*, *Home Alone*, and *Bad Santa*, and even gives viewers a nice Easter egg with the names "Farkus and Dill" shown on the side of the catering van the mercenaries use to infiltrate the compound—this of course being a reference to the bullies in another classic, *A Christmas Story*.

3

Silent Night, Scary Night

HORROR, THRILLER, AND SUSPENSE

As the winter solstice approaches each year, it brings with it the darkest and longest nights. It's a time when a distinct chill fills the air and a silent night becomes the perfect setting for spine-tingling cinematic experiences. Enter the perfect subgenre for those of us who never want Halloween to end: the Christmas horror movie.

Christmas horror movies embrace and amplify the season's inherent shadowy undertones. Here, the fire crackling in the hearth isn't the only thing slowly dying, prices aren't the only thing being slashed, and the line "last Christmas I gave you my heart" has a whole new meaning. If you're the type of person who likes your gift giver to be a demonic horned being that unleashes killer toys on its victims, then it's time to hang those monogrammed stockings and snuggle up for a visual onslaught of merry macabre that'll have you singing "killers and creatures and ghosts, oh my!" in no time.

Anna and the Apocalypse

Year: 2017

Director: John McPhail

Writers: Alan McDonald, Ryan McHenry

Cast: Ella Hunt, Malcolm Cumming, Sarah Swire, Mark Benton, Paul Kaye

Plot: When a zombie apocalypse disrupts the Scottish town of Little Haven at Christmas, Anna and her friends find themselves battling the flesh-eating undead (through song and dance).

Cheer-O-Meter

Christmas Spirit

Warm Fuzzies

Timelessness

1. While being driven to school by her widowed father, Anna upsets him when she announces she's skipping university to take a year off in what country?

    A. America

    B. France

    C. Australia

    D. Iceland

2. Anna's friend John wears an ugly Christmas sweater throughout all the carnage with what light-up design?

   A. Christmas tree

   B. Christmas ornaments

   C. Santa and reindeer

   D. Gingerbread house

3. On their morning walk to school, Anna and John finally realize there's a zombie outbreak. The first zombie they encounter is dressed as Frosty the Snowman, and Anna uses what playground fixture to kill him?

   A. Swing

   B. Seesaw

   C. Slide

   D. Spinner

4. When the army gets overrun with zombies, Anna, John, Chris, and Steph are saved by kill-happy Nick and his friends. They all get ambushed at a Christmas tree outlet and shopping mall where what character sacrifices themself to save Anna?

   A. Tony

   B. Steph

   C. Chris

   D. John

5. Many different weapons are used throughout the course of the film, from video game controllers to watermelons to bowling balls. What two signature weapons are wielded by Nick and Anna?

   A. Cricket bat / tennis racket

   B. Fireplace poker / sledgehammer

   C. Baseball bat / candy-cane lawn ornament

   D. Axe / ice skate

Festive Fact

All the original music was written by Scottish musicians and songwriters Roddy Hart and Tommy Reilly. After the film, the dynamic duo went on to write songs for the revival of Steven Spielberg's *Animaniacs*.

6. The survivors reach the high school, where unpopular teacher Mr. Savage is having a sadistic power trip, letting all his students get attacked on purpose. What item does he use to sic the zombies on his students?

A. Triangle

B. Whistle

C. Intercom

D. Bullhorn

7. After Anna saves her father, Tony, from Mr. Savage, Tony and the teacher fight until what stage prop from the Christmas show takes Mr. Savage out?

A. A Christmas gnome

B. A nutcracker

C. Santa's sleigh

D. A Christmas star

8. Nick and Anna manage to escape the auditorium only to be surrounded by a bunch of zombies. When all hope is lost, what character arrives in the nick of time to save them?

A. John with army reserves

B. Tony in a double-decker bus

C. Steph in her car

D. Chris and Lisa in an ambulance

Festive Fact

The film was shot in twenty-eight days in and around Port Glasgow in Scotland.

ANSWERS: 1.C, 2.A, 3.B, 4.D, 5.C, 6.B, 7.D, 8.C

Black Christmas

Year: 1974

Director: Bob Clark

Writer: Roy Moore

Cast: Olivia Hussey, Keir Dullea, Margot Kidder, John Saxon, Andrea Martin

Plot: This tale of terror takes place over Christmas break in a sorority house, where the sisters begin receiving unsettling and obscene phone calls from a mysterious stalker. Holiday cheer turns to horror when, one by one, girls start disappearing.

Cheer-O-Meter

Christmas Spirit

Warm Fuzzies

Timelessness

1. The film opens to the Christmas carol "O Holy Night" and an image of a festively decorated house belonging to what sorority that is the subject of the film?

   A. Theta Phi Alpha

   B. Kappa Phi Lambda

   C. Pi Kappa Sigma

   D. Kappa Mu Epsilon

Festive Fact

Comedy legend Gilda Radner was originally offered the part of Phyl, Jess's friend. She had to drop out one month before shooting due to her other commitment, *Saturday Night Live*.

SILENT NIGHT, SCARY NIGHT

2. After grudgingly agreeing to wear the ugly nightgown the girls got her as a Christmas present, housemother Mrs. Mac lets off steam by pulling a string inside the toilet tank to access a secret stash of what?

A. Chocolate

B. Liquor

C. Cigarettes

D. Hard candies

3. Jess reveals to her boyfriend, Peter, that she's pregnant, and the stress of the news weighs on him to the point that his recital goes awry. What instrument does he play?

A. Cello

B. Violin

C. French horn

D. Piano

4. For the entire film, Clare's body is shown propped up in a rocking chair in the attic by the window. What character is the first to find her up there?

A. Mrs. Mac

B. Claude the cat

C. Barb

D. Phyl

5. Barb was sent to bed after telling a crass story about a turtle to Clare's grieving father. She meets her untimely end with what unusual weapon?

A. A snowflake ornament

B. A picture frame

C. A glass unicorn statue

D. A candle

Festive Fact

Steve Martin is a huge fan of *Black Christmas*; he reportedly told Olivia Hussey, who played Jess, that he'd seen the film twenty-three times.

6. A group of carolers come to the house while the killer is loose within. Jess meets them at the door and listens to them sing what Christmas carol?

   A. "O Come, All Ye Faithful"

   B. "O Little Town of Bethlehem"

   C. "O Come, O Come, Emmanuel"

   D. "O Christmas Tree"

7. Lieutenant Fuller tells Jess that he will trace the call to find out where the killer is located. After several failed attempts and a dead police officer, where do Fuller and his team find the killer is calling from?

   A. Peter's music conservatory

   B. The police station

   C. Bedford retirement home

   D. Inside the house

8. *Black Christmas* was one of the first of a handful of films to depict a "Final Girl"—or last surviving woman—who confronts the killer and ends the story. What is her name?

   A. Phyl

   B. Laurie

   C. Jess

   D. Sally

Gremlins

Year: 1984

Director: Joe Dante

Writer: Chris Columbus

Cast: Zach Galligan, Phoebe Cates, Hoyt Axton, Frances Lee McCain, Polly Holliday

Plot: In this cult classic, a traveling salesman buys his son, Billy, a mysterious creature called a mogwai for Christmas. When Billy disregards its special-handling instructions, the creature spawns malevolent gremlins that wreak havoc.

Cheer-O-Meter

Christmas Spirit

Warm Fuzzies

Timelessness

1. **Billy is given all but which of the following rules for the mogwai?**

   A. Keep him out of the light, especially sunlight

   B. Never feed him after midnight

   C. Keep him away from extreme temperatures

   D. Keep him away from water. Don't get him wet

2. **Mrs. Deagle, the town's widowed miser, threatens to kill Billy's dog, Barney, after he decapitated what Christmas decoration of hers?**

   A. Imported Romanian reindeer

   B. Imported Hungarian Santa

   C. Imported Bulgarian nutcracker

   D. Imported Bavarian snowman

POP CORN

3. Kate is trying to get people to sign a petition to make what Kingston Falls bar a landmark so Mrs. Deagle can't take its lease away?

    A. Dorry's Tavern

    B. Nemo's Tavern

    C. Declan's Tavern

    D. Ed's Tavern

4. What was Billy's mother doing while the cocoons in the house were hatching?

    A. Decorating the Christmas tree

    B. Wrapping Christmas presents

    C. Making gingerbread cookies

    D. Playing Solitaire

5. What is the only brand of snowplow that Mr. Futterman, the town's snowplow driver and xenophobic WWII vet, trusts?

    A. Kansas City Harvester

    B. Knoxville Harvester

    C. Kenosha Harvester

    D. Kentucky Harvester

6. Where does Spike, the mohawked leader of the gremlins, go for enough water so he can multiply into a gremlin army?

    A. He jumps in the pool at the YMCA

    B. He jumps in the high school showers

    C. He jumps in the pond by the clock tower

    D. He jumps in the town fountain

7. After escaping the bar, Billy and Kate track hundreds of gremlins to the town's movie theater, where they are watching what movie?

    A *Gone with the Wind*

    B. *Casablanca*

    C. *Snow White and the Seven Dwarfs*

    D. *The Wizard of Oz*

8. During the finale, Billy and Kate confront Spike at the town's Montgomery Ward department store, but Gizmo saves the day in what heroic fashion?

    A. Riding on the back of Barney

    B. Zip-lining from a telephone pole

    C. Parachuting through the window

    D. Driving a pink electric toy Corvette

ANSWERS: 1.C, 2.D, 3.A, 4.C, 5.D, 6.A, 7.C, 8.D

Krampus

Year: 2015

Director: Michael Dougherty

Writers: Todd Casey, Michael Dougherty, Zach Shields

Cast: Adam Scott, Toni Collette, David Koechner, Allison Tolman, Conchata Ferrell

Plot: Thanks to his dysfunctional family's squabbling, young Max loses his belief in Santa Claus, inadvertently summoning the ancient demon Krampus, who punishes badly behaved children and those who've lost the Christmas spirit.

Cheer-O-Meter

Christmas Spirit

Warm Fuzzies

Timelessness

1. After a fight, Max confides in his grandmother, Omi, that the other boy said Santa was a marketing ploy. What language does Omi primarily speak throughout the film?

   A. Hungarian

   B. German

   C. Romanian

   D. Icelandic

2. What do Stevie and Jordan, Max's masculine cousins, do at dinner to humiliate him in front of everyone, leading Max to denounce Christmas?

   A. Pants him, revealing reindeer boxers

   B. Spill his food all over him

   C. Read his letter to Santa out loud

   D. Call him a "baby believer"

3. Beth, worried about her boyfriend, braves the blizzard to go check on him. After she hides under a DHL truck, she is attacked by what Christmas toy Krampus puts on the ground?

    a. Jack-in-the-box

    b. Russian nesting dolls

    c. Monkey with cymbals

    d. Wind-up metal Krampus

4. Tom and Howard arm themselves and look for Beth but are attacked by an unseen snow monster. When they return to Howard's Hummer and find that it's destroyed, Howard screams what nickname for it?

    A. Melinda

    B. Yolanda

    C. Glinda

    D. Lucinda

5. The remaining survivors follow Tom's lead to try to find the abandoned snowplow. Which family member stays behind to face Krampus one-on-one, who arrives to the tune of "Up on the Housetop" on the radio?

    A. Howard

    B. Omi

    C. Max

    D. Rosie the dog

Festive Fact

The snow on the ground was mostly made from polymers, a material that's usually reserved for diapers.

6. Everyone is attacked, taken, or presumably killed except for Max, who comes face-to-face with Krampus. The horned figure gives Max what item wrapped in the ripped-up letter to Santa that he discarded out the window earlier that night?

   A. His family's Christmas photo

   B. Omi's necklace

   C. A bloody candy cane

   D. An ornament

7. On Christmas morning, the family slowly begins to remember the horrors of the previous night before viewers are shown that Krampus is watching them from his lair filled with what item?

   A. Jack-in-the-boxes

   B. Elf masks

   C. Snow globes

   D. Chains

8. Finish the quote from Omi:
   "Krampus came not to reward but to _____.
   Not to ____ but to ____."

   A. Punish/give/take

   B. Discipline/love/hate

   C. Avenge/save/sacrifice

   D. Devour/spare/curse

Festive Fact

Two of the evil gingerbread men are voiced by Seth Green and *Rick and Morty* voice actor Justin Roiland.

ANSWERS: 1.B, 2.C, 3.A, 4.D, 5.B, 6.D, 7.C, 8.A

Disney Tim Burton's The Nightmare Before Christmas

Cheer-O-Meter

Christmas Spirit

Warm Fuzzies

Timelessness

Year: 1993

Director: Henry Selick

Writer: Caroline Thompson (adaptation by Michael McDowell)

Cast: Danny Elfman, Chris Sarandon, Catherine O'Hara, William Hickey, Glenn Shadix

Plot: Jack Skellington, the Pumpkin King of Halloween Town, visits the enchanting world of Christmas Town and is captivated by its joy and wonder. When Jack decides to bring Christmas back to his spooky realm, his well-intentioned plans go awry.

1. The Pumpkin King of Halloween Town, Jack Skellington, finds himself in a clearing containing magical doors on trees, each of which leads to fantasy worlds for all but which of the following holidays?

    A. St. Patrick's Day

    B. Valentine's Day

    C. New Year's Day

    D. Easter

2. Sally often poisons Dr. Finkelstein with what toxic ingredient?

    A. Deadly nightshade

    B. Newt saliva

    C. Shadow orchid

    D. Spectral toadstool

3. Sitting all alone, Sally picks a dead flower's petals, leading to a vision of the flower transforming into what festive item that catches fire and burns to a crisp?

    A. A Christmas present

    B. A Christmas stocking

    C. A Christmas ornament

    D. A Christmas tree

4. Oogie Boogie's favorite trio of trick-or-treaters travel by walking bathtub to go and kidnap "Sandy Claws" for Jack. What are the names of these three mischievous, mask-wearing children?

    A. Lock, Shock, and Barrel

    B. Pop, Rock, and Andy

    C. Jolt, Jinx, and Rattle

    D. Rumble, Jumble, and Switch

5. As Jack prepares to become his own version of Santa, a fog thicker than jellied brains permeates the skies of Halloween Town. Jack tasks his loyal ghost dog companion to light the way. What is the dog's name?

    A. Shadow

    B. Skull

    C. Phantom

    D. Zero

Festive Fact

Danny Elfman, film composer and former front man of Oingo Boingo, provided music and lyrics for the film. Elfman also was the singing voice for Jack Skellington.

6. Before Sally and Santa are ultimately saved from Oogie Boogie by Jack, what does Sally try to distract the boogeyman with when attempting to release Santa?

    A. A poisonous potion

    B. A kiss

    C. An enticing-looking bug

    D. Her detached leg

7. In his casket sleigh, Jack starts to deliver Christmas toys more suited for Halloween Town and is mocking and mangling the joyous holiday. He's shot down by a rocket and lands in what apropos location?

    A. A swamp

    B. A cemetery

    C. An insane asylum

    D. A pumpkin patch

8. Santa eventually returns to his post and, at supersonic speed, sets things right by bringing joy and cheer to children around the world. He also gifts Halloween Town with what "Christmas thing"?

    A. Snowfall across Halloween Town

    B. Bat-infested Christmas trees

    C. A batch of evil snowmen

    D. Cockroach Christmas cookies

Festive Fact

In a fun Easter egg, you'll find Jack Skellington's head on top of the carousel hat that Beetlejuice wears while saying "Attention Kmart shoppers" in Tim Burton's 1988 film *Beetlejuice*, which came out five years earlier.

ANSWERS: 1.C, 2.A, 3.D, 4.A, 5.D, 6.D, 7.B, 8.A

SPOTLIGHT QUIZ

Rare Exports: A Christmas Tale

Year: 2010

Director: Jalmari Helander

Writer: Jalmari Helander

Cast: Onni Tommila, Jorma Tommila, Per Christian Ellefsen, Tommi Korpela, Rauno Juvonen

Based on two popular short films from director Jalmari Helander, *Rare Exports: A Christmas Tale* quickly gained cult classic status in the United States and abroad thanks to its unconventional take on Santa Claus that brilliantly wove together Finnish legend and modern blockbuster filmmaking in a way that is accessible to a global audience. Blending horror, fantasy, and dark humor elements (with a touching father-son relationship amidst a fantastical premise), *Rare Exports* serves as a compelling reminder that horror knows no borders. It transcends cultural and linguistic divides and shows how a film deeply rooted in its own culture and folklore and in a different language can still resonate globally in service of one goal: a good scare.

Cheer-O-Meter

Christmas Spirit

Warm Fuzzies

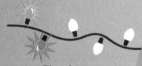

Timelessness

1. **Two young boys, Pietari and Juuso, snoop around Korvatunturi Mountain, believed to hold the frozen corpse of Santa Claus. Pietari goes home to investigate in what book that depicts Santa as a horned creature who punishes naughty children?**

   A. *The Legend of Santa Claus*

   B. *The Truth about Santa Claus*

   C. *A History of Santa Claus*

   D. *The First Santa Claus*

2. Over Christmas, the villagers become perplexed when certain items start going missing (along with their children), but no one is quite sure what is going on. All but which of the following items go missing?

   A. A hair dryer

   B. Potato sacks

   C. Slippers

   D. Radiators

3. The elves in this movie are old, naked men with beards. They don't like being taunted with what food item?

   A. Candy canes

   B. Bûche de Noël

   C. Peppermint bark

   D. Gingerbread cookies

4. Pietari devises a plan to lure all the elves to the reindeer pen by dangling the kidnapped children from a helicopter cargo net. Rauno and Aimo blow up frozen Santa Claus, but before they do, they take what souvenir from him?

   A. A sleigh bell

   B. A piece of fabric from his coat

   C. His horns

   D. His Naughty and Nice List

5. The survivors take the captured elves and start a business training them to be mall Santas. How many elves does Pietari count that will net them upwards of $17 million?

   A. 198

   B. 200

   C. 224

   D. 275

A Christmas Crime Scene

When it comes to horror movies, you aren't worth your screams
if your deaths aren't creative. And in a Christmas horror movie, there's
even more pressure with a limited amount of festive weaponry.
Can you match the list of victims with the film in which they appear?

1. Victim #1 – Death by golden scepter

2. Victim #2 – Death by eggnog

3. Victim #3 – Death by fiery explosion

4. Victim #4 – Death by flying paint can

5. Victim #5 – Death by Christmas lights

A. *Santa's Slay* (2005)

B. *Silent Night, Deadly Night* (1984)

C. *A Christmas Horror Story* (2015)

D. *P2* (2007)

E. *Better Watch Out* (2016)

ANSWERS: 1.C, 2.A, 3.D, 4.E, 5.B

POST-CREDITS

⭐ *Black Christmas* director Bob Clark was known for switching genres with his projects. After this slasher, he directed the comedy classic *Porky's* and, almost a decade after *Black Christmas*, returned to the holiday genre to direct another classic, **A Christmas Story**.

⭐ The central location of Kingston Falls in **Gremlins** (a play on *It's a Wonderful Life*'s Bedford Falls) is the same Universal Studios backlot used for Hill Valley in *Back to the Future*.

⭐ Despite the placement of Tim Burton's name above the title for **Disney Tim Burton's The Nightmare Before Christmas**, he did not direct the film. His former Disney animation colleague and friend Henry Selick was director of the film, with Burton serving as producer and providing the story based off his poem of the same name.

SILENT NIGHT, SCARY NIGHT

Stocking Stuffer

Christmas around the World

Every year, our yuletide movie-watching routine is packed to the brim, but like with Christmas dinner (and unbuttoning that top button) there's always room for more. While Hollywood has given us numerous classics over the past century, there is a rich array of Christmas films from other cultures. This Stocking Stuffer offers ten questions on films with international icons, acclaimed directors, and fresh spins on Christmas movie favorites that help solidify the fact that the true gift of Christmas will always be the same, but it's not a bad idea to change the way it's wrapped.

A Christmas Tale (2008), France

On Christmas Day, Elizabeth opens up to her father, Abel, about why she is so depressed. Abel reads the prologue to *On the Genealogy of Morality* written by what "God is dead" German philosopher?

A Not So Merry Christmas (2022), Mexico

Before Chuy goes on a tirade on Christmas Eve (also his birthday) about how the holiday is for parasites and mooches, the family does a gift exchange with dice, a variant of Yankee Swap, a party game better known by what colorful animal name?

Christmas Story (2007), Finland

In this touching origin story of Santa Claus, Nikolas becomes orphaned after his parents are killed in an accident. When a village takes him in, he gifts them toys made from what form of woodcarving that comes from the Middle English word for knife?

Fanny and Alexander (1982), Sweden

This is one of only three films from Sweden to ever win the Oscar for Best International Feature Film, all of which were helmed by what director of this film and beloved *Persona* of cinema?

Plácido (1961), Spain

During a Christmas campaign inspiring residents to break bread with the less fortunate, organizers hire Plácido and his motorcycle cart adorned with what roof decoration?

Joyeux Noel (2005), France

This film is a fictionalized account of the Christmas truce, an unofficial ceasefire during World War I around Christmas 1914, when French, German, and British soldiers put down their weapons, sang carols, and played an impromptu game of what?

Just Another Christmas (2020), Brazil

Jorge learns some troubling news about his daughter and finally agrees to her request to watch her favorite movie, a DreamWorks animation Christmas special with what title?

Love Is All (2007), Netherlands

Inspired by *Love Actually*, this film follows the lives of intersecting couples in Amsterdam on the days leading up to December 5th, also known as Saint Nicholas's eve, when what figure delivers presents to residents?

Tokyo Godfathers (2003), Japan

Finding an abandoned newborn on the streets of Tokyo on Christmas Eve are three homeless people, including a trans woman and former drag queen, Hana, who is adept at what seventeen-syllable poetic artform?

Vacanze di Natale (1983), Italy

Two families from different socioeconomic backgrounds collide in Cortina d'Ampezzo, an Italian resort town where Christmas holiday visitors can participate in what activity?

ANSWERS: 1. Friedrich Nietzsche, 2. White Elephant, 3. Whittling, 4. Ingmar Bergman, 5. Shooting star, 6. Soccer, 7. *Shrek the Halls*, 8. Sinterklaas, 9. Haiku, 10. Skiing

Up on the Rooftop
SANTA ON-SCREEN

We all have our own ideas of what Santa Claus should look like. Maybe it's inspired by the iconic Coca-Cola illustrations that shaped the modern look of Santa Claus, or perhaps it's influenced by a combination of mall Santas and family stories. Thankfully, Hollywood has treated us to a variety of cinematic Santas in all shapes and sizes—okay, mostly one shape.

We've seen Santa fight Martians, battle mercenaries, raise a human elf, and teach us about the line of succession. We've debated all his magical details and picked our favorite owner of the iconic red suit. Each version of Old St. Nick, whether steeped in tradition or sprinkled with modern twists, invites viewers of all ages to believe in magic and suspend their disbelief for at least one important question: How does he deliver all those presents in one night? So, grab the cookies, pour the milk, and enjoy a peek behind the North Pole curtain as we settle in for an enchanting sleigh ride through the world of Christmas movies featuring the most beloved character of all: Santa Claus.

Fred Claus

Year: 2007

Director: David Dobkin

Writer: Dan Fogelman

Cast: Vince Vaughn, Paul Giamatti, Elizabeth Banks, John Michael Higgins, Rachel Weisz

Plot: When Fred Claus, Santa's bitter and estranged older brother, faces financial troubles, he is invited to live at the North Pole, where he struggles with the elves and his own personal shortcomings. But when Christmas is threatened, Fred steps in to help.

Cheer-O-Meter

Christmas Spirit

Warm Fuzzies

Timelessness

NORTH POLE

1. If the titular character played by Vince Vaughn had a Christmas file on Santa's desk describing specific details about his life, which one of the following would be incorrect?

A. He's a Chicago repo man who hates Christmas

B. He loves knocking down children's snowmen

C. He's in an on-again, off-again relationship with a British meter maid

D. He's a schemer who particularly loves stealing from Salvation Army Santas

2. Efficiency expert Mr. Northcutt has already canceled the Easter Bunny. His quest to outsource Christmas to the South Pole is thwarted by Santa, who cures his resting Grinch face with what special gift?

   A. A Superman cape

   B. A Teddy Ruxpin

   C. A vintage Sony Walkman

   D. A Radio Flyer Classic Red Wagon

3. Donnie, the North Pole's premiere DJ, played by rapper Ludacris, loves to roll out what Christmas song, on repeat, driving Fred to madness?

   A. "Little Saint Nick"

   B. "Santa Claus Is Coming to Town"

   C. "Here Comes Santa Claus"

   D. "Rapper's Delight"

4. Fred goes to a Siblings Anonymous meeting to try to grapple with the responsibility of being the brother of Santa Claus. There, he learns some valuable lessons from what other real-life sibling?

   A. Roger Clinton, brother of President Bill Clinton

   B. Frank Stallone, brother of Sylvester Stallone

   C. Stephen Baldwin, brother of Alec Baldwin

   D. All of the above

5. Fred returns to the North Pole to rally the elves to meet their quota guaranteeing every child a present on Christmas Day. The rule states that only a Claus can deliver presents, so Fred delivers what two gifts to all the children of the world?

   A. Baseball bat / Hula-Hoop

   B. Etch A Sketch / Easy Bake Oven

   C. Bicycle / Rollerblades

   D. Karaoke machine / skateboard

6. After witnessing Slam acting out at his orphanage, Fred does what extreme action that causes seemingly irrevocable damage to the Christmas operation and gives Mr. Northcutt ammo to shut it down?

   A. Brings Slam to the North Pole

   B. Labels every child's file "nice"

   C. Turns off the electricity to the toy factory

   D. Makes a fake Naughty or Nice List

7. Fred teaches Head Elf Willie how to dance to the song "Beast of Burden" by the Rolling Stones, giving Willie the "elf-esteem" to profess his love to which resident of the North Pole?

   A. Bethany, North Pole flight commander

   B. Katherine, head of wrapping

   C. Charlene, Santa's little helper

   D. Dina, postmaster general

8. While his true Christmas gift to Wanda is reforming his past tendencies, Fred also gives her a teddy bear and takes her on a special sleigh ride to where?

   A. To the North Pole

   B. Around the Eiffel Tower

   C. Over the Roman Colosseum

   D. Across the Grand Canyon

Festive Fact

At the time the film was released, it featured five Oscar nominees or winners, including Miranda Richardson (Annette Claus), Paul Giamatti (Nick), Rachel Weisz (Wanda), Kathy Bates (Mother Claus), and Kevin Spacey (Clyde).

Miracle on 34th Street

Year: 1947

Director: George Seaton

Writer: George Seaton (story by Valentine Davies)

Cast: Edmund Gwenn, Maureen O'Hara, John Payne, Natalie Wood, Porter Hall

Plot: Kris Kringle, a kind old man working at Macy's, asserts that he is the real Santa Claus, igniting a sensational court case in New York City. As belief and skepticism clash, lawyer Fred Gailey defends Kris's identity and reawakens the true spirit of Christmas in New Yorkers' hearts.

1. **Doris Walker first meets Kris Kringle as she helps organize the Macy's Thanksgiving Day Parade. Kris complains that the current Macy's Santa is unable to do his duties for what reason?**

   A. He wears a fake beard

   B. Cupid, Blitzen, and Donner were in the wrong position

   C. He was intoxicated and is a disgrace to the tradition of Christmas

   D. His costume was the wrong shade of red

Cheer-O-Meter

Christmas Spirit

Warm Fuzzies

Timelessness

Festive Fact

The scenes of the Macy's Thanksgiving Day Parade were entirely real, shot on location in freezing temperatures at the 1946 parade. Actor Edmund Gwenn actually played the parade Santa Claus himself.

2. **Doris asks Kris to explain to her daughter, Susan, that he really isn't Santa Claus. But Kris stands firm, so Doris grabs his employment card and is shocked to see that his date of birth is listed as what?**

   A. As old as my tongue and a little bit older than my teeth

   B. January 1st

   C. You'll have to ask Dasher, Dancer, Prancer, or Vixen

   D. A Kringle never reveals his age

3. **The first child that meets Kris as Macy's Santa Claus asks for a specific gift, but when Kris says he shall have it, his mother says that nobody is selling it. What was the gift?**

   A. A Tonka truck with a fully functional crane and clam

   B. An electric train with a long track that has real smoke

   C. A holster filled with western six-shooters and a sheriff badge

   D. A fire engine with a real hose that squirts real water

4. **Kris inspires Macy's to adopt a merchandising policy where, if they don't have an item, they send customers to a store that does. Mr. Macy loves it and even shakes hands with what major competitor?**

   A. Hearn's

   B. Gimbels

   C. Schoenfeld's

   D. Bloomingdale's

5. **In a memorable and heartwarming scene, Kris impresses Susan by communicating with a recently adopted young girl who only speaks what language? (In the remake, it's changed to American Sign Language.)**

   A. Dutch

   B. German

   C. Icelandic

   D. Lithuanian

6. During the court hearing on Christmas Eve, what definitive piece of evidence does Fred Gailey use, in dramatic fashion, to provide the court authoritative proof that Kris Kringle is the one and only Santa Claus?

A. Testimony from Thomas Mara Jr. (the prosecutor's young son)

B. The real, genuine Naughty and Nice List

C. Letters addressed to "Santa Claus" delivered by the US Postal Service

D. A phone call from the president of the United States

Festive Fact

The National Legion of Decency gave the movie a B rating for being "morally objectionable" due to the film's depiction of a divorced mother.

7. During a Christmas Party, Kris upsets Susan when he doesn't deliver her special gift request. Doris consoles her and repeats the following quote from Fred. Can you complete the quote? "Faith is believing in things when _____"

A. You can't see them

B. Everyone tells you not to

C. Common sense tells you not to

D. Every fiber of your being tells you not to

8. The iconic final image of the film shows what item that convinces Doris and Fred that Kris Kringle is in fact Santa Claus?

A. A Santa hat

B. A cane

C. A letter from Kris

D. Boot prints

Santa Claus: The Movie

Year: 1985

Director: Jeannot Szwarc

Writer: David Newman (story by David Newman and Leslie Newman)

Cast: Dudley Moore, John Lithgow, David Huddleston, Judy Cornwell, Burgess Meredith

Plot: An ambitious toy tycoon in New York City tempts Santa's head elf with a vision for Christmas commercialization that threatens the holiday. This origin story follows Santa from simple toymaker to beloved bringer of Christmas joy.

Cheer-O-Meter

Christmas Spirit

Warm Fuzzies

Timelessness

1. Before he becomes Santa Claus, he's just a woodworker named Claus. Every Christmas, he brings hand-carved toys to the children of his village accompanied by his wife, Anya, and what two reindeer?

   A. Dasher and Prancer

   B. Donner and Blitzen

   C. Comet and Vixen

   D. Cupid and Dancer

2. Upon being transported to the North Pole, Claus and Anya are introduced to Dooly and Patch, who prefer to be called elves rather than what name used in Claus's village?

   A. Vendora

   B. Vendeloo

   C. Vendegum

   D. Vendevoo

3. What color was Santa Claus's iconic outfit before Anya says it isn't really his color?

    A. Green

    B. Blue

    C. Purple

    D. Gold

4. Santa makes a pit stop for an orphan named Joe and takes him for a ride in his sleigh. They try to do what vertical-loop maneuver with Donner, which fails due to the reindeer's fear of heights?

    A. Super Duper Looper

    B. Mega Twirl Whirl

    C. Spiral Swirl Twirl

    D. Looping Scoopenator

5. Santa and Joe deliver presents to Cornelia, who tells Santa that he can have some cookies from which famous New York City department store?

    A. Macy's

    B. Saks Fifth Avenue

    C. Bergdorf Goodman

    D. Bloomingdale's

6. Patch, Santa's new assistant, resigns after his automated system produced shoddy toys. He leaves the North Pole and mistakenly joins what disgraced company run by Cornelia's amoral step-uncle?

    A. E.Z. Toy Company

    B. D.Z. Toy Company

    C. T.Z. Toy Company

    D. B.Z. Toy Company

7. Patch develops what treat (filled with the same magic dust the reindeer eat to fly) that he delivers on Christmas Eve? The treat becomes an instant sensation because it makes people fly but also makes Santa feel obsolete.

    A. Cookies

    B. Hot cocoa

    C. Lollipops

    D. Gumdrops

8. When Patch saves Joe, who has been tied up by Cornelia's uncle, what is Joe carrying that ultimately helps Patch realize Santa still cares for him?

    A. A letter from Santa in Joe's pocket

    B. Joe gives him one of Santa's magic sleigh bells

    C. He notices that Joe's wooden toy sculpture is Patch's elf portrait

    D. Dasher's harness

The Christmas Chronicles

Year: 2018

Director: Clay Kaytis

Writer: Matt Lieberman (story by Matt Lieberman and David Guggenheim)

Cast: Kurt Russell, Darby Camp, Judah Lewis, Lamorne Morris, Kimberly Williams-Paisley

Plot: While trying to prove the existence of Santa Claus on Christmas Eve, siblings Kate and Teddy stow away on Santa's sleigh and inadvertently cause it to crash, sparking a wild race against time to save Christmas.

Cheer-O-Meter

Christmas Spirit

Warm Fuzzies

Timelessness

1. Kate loves to carry around what beloved item belonging to her late father? She has it when Teddy steals a car, when Santa first arrives at their house, and when she meets all the elves at the North Pole.

    A. His firefighter badge

    B. His New England Patriots pen

    C. His Sony Handycam

    D. His wallet photo of the family

Festive Fact

While being interrogated, Santa Claus tries to impress Officer Dave Poveda with toys he wanted as a child, including a *Star Wars* Han Solo action figure. Kurt Russell auditioned for Han Solo, but it went to some other guy.

2. Kate and Teddy stow away on Santa's sleigh, startling him and causing an epic disaster that releases the reindeer and forces Santa to make an emergency landing in what city nearly a thousand miles away?

   A. Detroit
   B. Chicago
   C. Milwaukee
   D. Cleveland

3. When Santa, Kate, and Teddy are in serious need of some transportation, Santa tries bribing a dinner patron named Larry for access to his Porsche by offering him a mint-condition 1952 rookie card of what athlete?

   A. Warren Spahn
   B. Frank Gifford
   C. Jackie Robinson
   D. Mickey Mantle

4. What proof does Officer Dave Poveda get that fully convinces him he has locked up the real Santa Claus, leading him to release Santa in time to save Christmas?

   A. He sees a flying reindeer
   B. He sees the Christmas spirit meter
   C. The jail becomes full of troublemakers
   D. His ex-wife calls him to have coffee

5. What family mantra is inscribed on Teddy's knife that helps him believe in himself enough to get Santa's reindeer to fly over an oncoming train?

   A. A Pierce never gives up

   B. A Pierce always sees it through

   C. A Pierce never surrenders

   D. A Pierce always perseveres

6. While on the run searching for Santa's bag of toys, Kate and Teddy are inspired to stop when they hear what Christmas carol being sung by a choir in a nearby church? (It's their late father's favorite.)

   A. "Silent Night"

   B. "O Come, All Ye Faithful"

   C. "Away in a Manger"

   D. "O Christmas Tree"

7. At the North Pole, Kate finds a surprising letter to Santa sent this year by Teddy. What does he ask for in his letter to Santa?

   A. To see his dad one last time

   B. A red Dodge Challenger

   C. For the Chicago Bears to win the Super Bowl

   D. A Fender Stratocaster

8. At the end of the film, we are introduced to Mrs. Claus, who is played by what actress that brings some serious Christmas star power and sass to the role?

   A. Melanie Griffith

   B. Goldie Hawn

   C. Cybill Shepherd

   D. Michelle Pfeiffer

The Santa Clause

Cheer-O-Meter

Christmas Spirit

Warm Fuzzies

Timelessness

Year: 1994

Director: John Pasquin

Writers: Leo Benvenuti, Steve Rudnick

Cast: Tim Allen, Judge Reinhold, Wendy Crewson, David Krumholtz, Peter Boyle

Plot: Scott Calvin accidentally causes Santa Claus to fall off his roof on Christmas Eve and unwittingly triggers "The Santa Clause," recruiting him to take Santa's place. With the help of his son, Charlie, Scott embraces his new role, which leads to an unexpected journey of self-discovery.

1. **Scott's cooking proves why you need a high-quality fire extinguisher in the kitchen. With Christmas dinner burned, Scott takes Charlie to what American institution?**

   A. IHOP

   B. Denny's

   C. Cracker Barrel

   D. Waffle House

Festive Fact

If you want to play a fun game every time you rewatch the film, keep an eye out for elves in human clothing in different locations like classrooms, parks, and crowds.

2. When Scott and Charlie discover that the real Santa Claus has fallen off their roof, Scott smacks his head on a magical ladder that appears on their front walkway. What company manufactured this ladder?

   A. The YuleStep Ladder Company

   B. The North Pole Ladder Company

   C. The Housetop Ladder Company

   D. The Rose Suchak Ladder Company

3. What is the name of the second-in-command elf who hates dry turkey, likes Neal's sweaters, and also calls Charlie "sport"?

   A. Bertrand

   B. Barnaby

   C. Bartholomew

   D. Bernard

4. Judy the elf makes one legendary cup of cocoa. "Not too hot, extra chocolate, shaken, not stirred." How long did it take Judy to perfect her own recipe?

   A. 1,200 years

   B. 1,000 years

   C. 800 years

   D. 600 years

5. The last straw for Laura and Neal with Scott's "Santa thing" is when they see him entertaining a long line of children asking for gifts at what extracurricular event of Charlie's?

   A. Basketball game

   B. Soccer game

   C. Flag football game

   D. Kickball game

6. Thinking that Charlie has been kidnapped, Laura and Neal call the police, who, later that night, arrest Scott when he and Charlie visit his house. What is the name for the squad of elves that breaks Santa out of jail?

    A. Earth Logistics Flight Squad

    B. Efficient Landing Flight Squad

    C. Elite Land and Air Flight Squad

    D. Effective Liberating Flight Squad

7. Which one of Santa's reindeer, who gifted Scott a nice rope just in case he fell off the roof, immediately forms a bond with Scott and Charlie?

    A. Cupid

    B. Prancer

    C. Comet

    D. Dasher

8. Laura and Neal eventually come around to Scott being Santa Claus. What really seals the deal is Scott giving them their gifts that got away. What gifts parachute down from the sleigh?

    A. The Dating Game / dancing ballerina whistle

    B. Mystery Date Game / Oscar Mayer wiener whistle

    C. Barbie Queen of the Prom Game / Puff 'N Toot train whistle

    D. Blind Date Game / whirly whistle

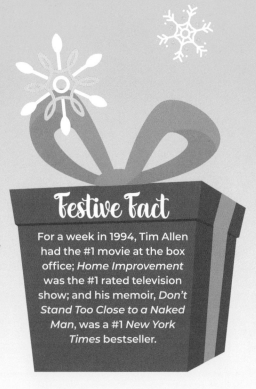

Festive Fact

For a week in 1994, Tim Allen had the #1 movie at the box office; *Home Improvement* was the #1 rated television show; and his memoir, *Don't Stand Too Close to a Naked Man*, was a #1 *New York Times* bestseller.

ANSWERS: 1.B, 2.D, 3.D, 4.A, 5.B, 6.D, 7.C, 8.B

The Santa Tracker

Each year, thanks to NORAD (North American Aerospace Defense Command), children across the globe can watch as Santa is tracked from the North Pole to all his stops around the world, giving gifts to children who have made the Nice List. Where in the world (or universe) was Santa Claus in these movies?

1. Planet Mars – 24.85, 213.25° W

2. Mexico City, Mexico - 19.4326° N, 99.1332° W

3. London, England - 51.5072° N, 0.1276° W

4. Los Angeles, CA - 34.0549° N, 118.2426° W

5. New York City, NY - 40.7128° N, 74.0060° W

A. *Get Santa* (2014)

B. *Call Me Claus* (2001) / *Santa Who?* (2000)

C. *Santa Claus Conquers the Martians* (1964)

D. *All I Want for Christmas* (1991)

E. *Santa Claus* (1959)

ANSWERS: 1.C, 2.E, 3.A, 4.B, 5.D

POST-CREDITS

★ Edmund Gwenn is the only actor who has won an Oscar for playing Kris Kringle. It makes sense, though, considering the fact that actress Natalie Wood (who played young Susan in *Miracle on 34th Street*) actually believed he was Santa Claus during filming until she saw him turn up at the wrap party with no beard.

★ In *The Christmas Chronicles*, the elvish language known as Yulish spoken by Santa, the elves, and quick learner Kate was invented by conlanger (language creator) David J. Peterson, who also created Dothraki and High Valyrian for *Game of Thrones*.

★ During the interrogation scene in *The Santa Clause* when an officer is asking Scott for his name (and he gives alternative names for Santa Claus), Scott at one point says "Topo Gigio," which is not an alias for Santa Claus but the name of an Italian mouse puppet often featured on *The Ed Sullivan Show*.

5

Comfort and Joy

FAMILY CHRISTMAS MOVIES

*C*lose your eyes and imagine you're a kid. If you already are one, channel your inner Peter Pan and never grow up. Picture yourself at home on a glorious snow day. You run down the stairs into the living room and see that your parents have set up a special family Christmas movie night. There are cozy blankets, matching candy-cane pajamas, hot cocoa with whipped cream in a Frosty the Snowman mug, and a bowl of buttered popcorn ready to be devoured. Isn't it just the greatest thing ever?

But how do you pick the perfect family Christmas movie? You need something visually engaging for little kids, filled with fun action or gags for teens, and, for adults, a few jokes that fly over the kids' heads, with a decent runtime to make sure everyone gets to bed on time. Most importantly, you need something that brings comfort and joy.

Every film in this chapter is either a certified classic, a new classic, or well on its way to becoming one. And no matter what movie you choose, these family bonding moments become fond memories to look back on and share with future generations.

Elf

Year: 2003

Director: Jon Favreau

Writer: David Berenbaum

Cast: Will Ferrell, James Caan, Zooey Deschanel, Mary Steenburgen, Ed Asner

Plot: In this modern classic, Buddy, a human raised by Santa's elves at the North Pole, discovers he's not a real elf and travels to New York City in search of his biological father for Christmas.

Cheer-O-Meter

Christmas Spirit

Warm Fuzzies

Timelessness

1. Before Buddy departs for New York City, he hears "Bye, Buddy. Hope you find your dad!" from what North Pole resident?

   A. Mr. Narwhal

   B. Walrus

   C. Leon the Snowman

   D. Arctic Puffin

2. Elves only have three jobs available to them: making shoes, baking cookies in trees, and making toys for Santa. But Papa Elf has an even more important job: narrator of this film. What iconic television star plays Papa Elf?

   A. Bob Denver

   B. Bob Hartley

   C. Bob Hope

   D. Bob Newhart

3. Due to being 915 off the pace for his Etch A Sketch quota, Buddy is sent to toy testing to be scared by jack-in-the-boxes and says, "I'm the worst toy maker in the world. I'm a _____". Complete the quote.

   A. Cotton-headed ninny blubbins

   B. Cotton-headed ninny puffins

   C. Cotton-headed ninny muggins

   D. Cotton-headed ninny muffins

4. Buddy leaves the North Pole to meet his father, Walter, who works for what publishing company inside the Empire State Building?

   A. Greenlight Press

   B. Greenway Press

   C. Greenstreet Press

   D. Greenville Press

5. He might have tasted the world's best cup of coffee, chugged two liters of Coke, and desperately wanted someone to eat sugar plums with him, but like all elves, Buddy sticks to what four main food groups?

   A. Candy, candy canes, candy corn, syrup

   B. Candy, candy corn, sugar, syrup

   C. Candy, cotton candy, maple syrup, sugar

   D. Candy, chocolate, cinnamon, peppermint

Festive Fact

When Buddy is walking around the city, he stops a man in a full red sweatsuit, thinking it's Santa. That just happened to be a random pedestrian, who is now a part of Christmas movie history.

6. What is the name of the famous children's book author (portrayed by *Game of Thrones* star Peter Dinklage) who Buddy irritates into a fight by calling him an elf multiple times?

   A. Miles Foster

   B. Miles Martin

   C. Miles Finch

   D. Miles Monroe

7. Ecstatic that Santa is coming to Gimbels, Buddy is angry when an imposter Santa shows up and confronts him in front of the children, saying he sits on a throne of lies and smells like what?

   A. Armpits and jelly

   B. Beef and cheese

   C. Onions and garlic

   D. Farts and feet

8. Trying to bond with his new brother, Michael, Buddy picks him up after school and together they partake in all but which of the following activities around New York City?

   A. A snowball fight in Central Park

   B. Jumping up and down on department store mattresses

   C. Cutting down a Christmas tree

   D. Speed running through revolving doors

Festive Fact

The manager of Gimbels (played by Faizon Love), who loves six-inch ribbon curls, wears a nametag labeled "Wanda" because comedian Wanda Sykes was initially cast in the role but had to drop out shortly before production.

ANSWERS: 1.A, 2.D, 3.C, 4.B, 5.A, 6.C, 7.B, 8.D

Home Alone

Year: 1990

Director: Chris Columbus

Writer: John Hughes

Cast: Macaulay Culkin, Joe Pesci, Daniel Stern, Roberts Blossom, Catherine O'Hara

Plot: This beloved holiday movie follows the adventures of Kevin McCallister, an eight-year-old boy who is accidentally left behind when his family jets off to Paris for Christmas. Kevin faces two bumbling burglars attempting to break in and defends his home by using his wit and a series of ingenious booby traps.

1. Kevin uses the audio from what fictional black-and-white James Cagney–inspired gangster film to scare away Marv (with help from some firecrackers) and the Little Nero's Pizza driver?

   A. *Angels with Dirty Faces*

   B. *Angels with Filthy Faces*

   C. *Angels with Filthy Souls*

   D. *Angels with Dirty Souls*

Cheer-O-Meter

Christmas Spirit

Warm Fuzzies

Timelessness

Festive Fact

The fictitious gangster film-within-a-film Kevin watches (which for many years Seth Rogen, Chris Evans, Nick Kroll, and Elijah Wood thought was real) was shot in one day on the final test day before official photography began. On set, it was known as "the gangster film" until filmmakers realized they needed a title written on the VHS. They settled on a nod to actor James Cagney.

COMFORT AND JOY

2. Kevin declares that he doesn't want to share a bed with his cousin Fuller (played by Culkin's real-life brother Kieran Culkin) because he wets the bed and will pee all over him. What drink does Fuller need to go easy on?

   A. Coke

   B. Dr Pepper

   C. Pepsi

   D. Mountain Dew

3. Set to the tune of "Rockin' around the Christmas Tree," Kevin sets up his living room to give the illusion that a massive party is taking place, using a cardboard cutout of what notable figure?

   A. Michael Jordan

   B. Arnold Schwarzenegger

   C. Bo Jackson

   D. Superman

4. Kevin pays a visit to a neighborhood Santa and asks him to deliver a message that all he wants for Christmas is his family back. Santa asks Kevin to hold out his little paw and gives him what gift?

   A. A broken candy cane

   B. A buy-one, get-one-free slushie coupon

   C. A stick of Fruit Stripe gum

   D. Three green Tic Tacs

5. Kevin becomes frightened at a store when he sees Old Man Marley, so he dashes out of the store with a toothbrush in hand and is chased by security. What information was Kevin trying to get from the clerk before he was scared away?

   A. If the toothbrush was approved by the American Dental Association

   B. If the toothbrush was on sale

   C. If the toothbrush was battery powered

   D. If the toothbrush came in blue because pink is for girls

6. When it comes to defeating burglars, eight-year-old Kevin is a genius-level booby-trap designer. Of the following traps set up for Harry and Marv, which one did Kevin NOT use on them?

   A. An electric barbecue starter on the front-door handle

   B. An iron triggered by a pull switch to fall down a laundry chute

   C. Plastic wrap covered in caulking glue which triggers feathers and a fan

   D. Frozen bricks wrapped in string and swung from the upper railing

7. Who displays the ultimate example of Christmas spirit by offering Kevin's mother, Kate, a ride from Scranton, Pennsylvania, to Chicago so she can get home to Kevin?

   A. Garth Volback, Beef King of Berwyn

   B. Gus Polinski, Polka King of the Midwest

   C. Abe Froman, Sausage King of Chicago

   D. Buck Russell, Pancake King of Kenosha

8. Before Kevin gazes out his window to see Old Man Marley tearfully reuniting with his family, his father, Peter, finds what item on the floor? It's the only clue left that Kevin went Rambo on a pair of house invaders.

   A. A gold tooth

   B. A crowbar

   C. A fake police badge

   D. A broken ornament

Festive Fact

The interiors were all built inside the gymnasium at New Trier Township High School in Winnetka, Illinois, the same school where scenes were shot for *Ferris Bueller's Day Off* and *Uncle Buck*. The scenes where Kevin walks through the neighbor's flooded house were achieved by building the set over the school's pool.

ANSWERS: 1.C, 2.C, 3.A, 4.D, 5.A, 6.D, 7.B, 8.A

Jingle All the Way

Year: 1996

Director: Brian Levant

Writer: Randy Kornfield

Cast: Arnold Schwarzenegger, Sinbad, Phil Hartman, Rita Wilson, Jake Lloyd

Plot: During the holiday-shopping chaos, workaholic father Howard Langston is on a quest to find the season's hottest toy, Turbo Man, for his son on Christmas Eve. His journey has him battling frenzied crowds, a crazed postman, a nosy neighbor, and an angry reindeer.

Cheer-O-Meter

Christmas Spirit

Warm Fuzzies

Timelessness

Festive Fact

The film was shot in the Minneapolis–St. Paul area of Minnesota, including the Mall of America. Several scenes were also shot in Los Angeles, including the Wintertainment Parade at Universal Studios Hollywood for more control.

THE MALL

1. Howard is always on the phone taking care of his number-one mattress customer. He's so busy, in fact, that he completely misses what important event?

   A. Christmas dinner

   B. Jamie's talent show

   C. Jamie's recital

   D. Jamie's karate graduation

COMFORT AND JOY

2. He's faithful. He's pink and furry. And he's a saber-toothed tiger. Despite no one actually liking him or wanting him, he's the only character still available in stores. What is the name of Turbo Man's sidekick?

   A. Scooter

   B. Booster

   C. Bruiser

   D. Slasher

3. In the Turbo Man television and cinematic universe, what is the name of Turbo Man's archenemy who causes Howard mischief during the finale?

   A. Tormentor

   B. Dementor

   C. Re-Animator

   D. Gigantor

4. Howard races across all of Minnesota to try to find a Turbo Man action figure. He forms an alliance of sorts with Myron, a disgruntled postal worker. Myron is desperate to get Turbo Man for his son because his own father failed to get him what toy?

   A. Red Ryder BB Gun

   B. Underwater G.I. Joe

   C. Johnny Seven O.M.A. (One Man Army)

   D. Stretch Armstrong

5. Lamenting over the day's events, Howard and Myron bond at a diner . . . that is, until a radio show announces that the first caller who completes what festive task will win a Turbo Man doll?

   A. Name all the gifts from "The Twelve Days of Christmas"

   B. Recite the names of Santa's reindeer

   C. Be the 10th caller

   D. Name one of the top-ten highest-grossing Christmas movies

6. Ted, a single father and Howard's annoying next-door neighbor, is heartbroken to learn that the head of what statue from his nativity scene is burnt to a crisp?

    A. Balthazar

    B. Melchior

    C. Gaspar

    D. Joseph

7. Which of these actors does NOT make a surprise appearance during the counterfeit Santa operation where Howard realizes he was duped with a fake Turbo Man?

    A. Jim Belushi

    B. Paul Wight

    C. Verne Troyer

    D. Tony Hawk

8. After all the antics, action, twists, and turns, which character actually ends up with the elusive special edition Turbo Man doll by the time the credits roll?

    A. Myron

    B. Howard

    C. Jamie

    D. Ted

ANSWERS: 1.D, 2.B, 3.B, 4.C, 5.B, 6.A, 7.D, 8.A

Festive Fact

Toy manufacturer Tiger Electronics produced 200,000 real Turbo Man action figures that were sold to the public. The small number in production was due to the quick turnaround.

Dr. Seuss' How the Grinch Stole Christmas

Cheer-O-Meter

Christmas Spirit

Warm Fuzzies

Timelessness

Year: 2000

Director: Ron Howard

Writers: Jeffrey Price, Peter S. Seaman

Cast: Jim Carrey, Taylor Momsen, Jeffrey Tambor, Christine Baranski, Molly Shannon

Plot: This live-action adaptation brings the beloved Dr. Seuss tale to life. The film explores themes of acceptance, the power of community, and the transformative nature of kindness wrapped in a visually stunning and whimsical Seussian world.

1. What celebrated actor and former cinematic villain provides the storybook narration for the film? (It took him only one day to record his lines.)

   A. James Earl Jones

   B. Alan Rickman

   C. Anthony Hopkins

   D. Douglas Rain

Festive Fact

The film's soundtrack has songs by Faith Hill and *NSYNC, two songs cowritten by Mariah Carey, and even a rap called "Grinch 2000" by Busta Rhymes featuring Jim Carrey.

COMFORT AND JOY

2. At the post office, Cindy Lou Who's father, Lou Lou Who, is under a lot of pressure from the residents of Whoville to deliver their gifts as fast as possible and often has to use what special form of shipping?

A. Heckuvarush

B. ASAWP (as soon as Who-manly possible)

C. Ship-Mas Miracle

D. Elf-X-Press

3. As a child, the Grinch has a crush on Martha May Whovier and makes her what special Christmas gift, a gesture that would solidify Martha May's crush on the Grinch, which clearly lasts into adulthood?

A. A metal Santa ornament

B. A metal reindeer statue

C. A metal decorative Christmas tree

D. A metal angel tree topper

4. Following a traumatic experience at school, an eight-year-old Grinch decides to isolate on what mountain, thousands of feet in the air, overlooking Whoville?

A. Mount Slumpit

B. Mount Lumpit

C. Mount Crumpit

D. Mount Blumpit

5. When invited to be Holiday Cheermeister for Whoville's one thousandth Whobilation, the Grinch is worried that his schedule won't allow it. Which of the following scheduled activities are NOT on his calendar?

   A. One o'clock, wallow in self-pity

   B. Four o'clock, Zumba followed by *The Golden Girls*

   C. Five o'clock, solve world hunger—tell no one

   D. Seven o'clock, wrestle with my self-loathing

6. The Grinch swings by the Whobilation fashionably late wearing what outfit?

   A. A kilt made out of a tablecloth

   B. A Santa outfit

   C. A Giorgi-Who Armani suit

   D. Lederhosen stolen from a yodeler

7. Humiliated once again by the Whos at Whobilation, the Grinch steals the town's presents and decorations while they sleep. He uses a high-tech sleigh with what license plate?

   A. Mean 1

   B. Green 1

   C. Gr1nch

   D. Vile 1

Festive Fact

Jim Carrey compared the makeup process of becoming the Grinch to being "buried alive" and considered quitting the movie because of it. It was so bad that to help Carrey cope, producers brought in a CIA instructor who taught operatives how to endure torture.

8. When the Grinch realizes the true meaning of Christmas, he redelivers all the presents. The whole town celebrates with a Christmas feast at the Grinch's home, where he performs what important task?

   A. He makes the Christmas toast

   B. He cooks the Christmas turkey

   C. He carves the roast beast

   D. He sings the first carol

Jingle Jangle: A Christmas Journey

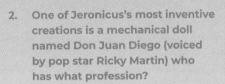

Cheer-O-Meter

Christmas Spirit

Warm Fuzzies

Timelessness

Year: 2020

Director: David E. Talbert

Writer: David E. Talbert

Cast: Forest Whitaker, Madalen Mills, Keegan-Michael Key, Anika Noni Rose, Phylicia Rashad

Plot: This musical adventure, brimming with imagination, follows legendary toymaker Jeronicus Jangle as he relearns the spirit of Christmas thanks to his inventive and brilliant granddaughter, Journey.

1. At the center of the story is a most magnificent shop run by Jeronicus that has the whole town abuzz. It has gadgets, gizmos, and the most spectacular inventions as far as the eye can see. What is the shop called?

   A. Jingle Jangle

   B. Jangles and Things

   C. Jingle and Joy

   D. Trinkets and Treasures

2. One of Jeronicus's most inventive creations is a mechanical doll named Don Juan Diego (voiced by pop star Ricky Martin) who has what profession?

   A. Luchador

   B. Singer

   C. Matador

   D. Flamenco dancer

3. What trusted and loyal apprentice of Jeronicus steals his book of inventions, propelling him to become a future twenty-eight-time Toymaker of the Year?

   A. Gunderson

   B. Gunnerson

   C. Gadson

   D. Gustafson

4. What is the name of the banker who tells Jeronicus he must create a revolutionary invention or pay his debts by Christmas to avoid the bank's seizure of the store's assets?

   A. Mr. Delacourte

   B. Mr. Delacroix

   C. Dr. LaCroix

   D. Ms. Desjardins

5. Jeronicus finally agrees to let his granddaughter stay after seeing an old photo of Jessica, his daughter and Journey's mother, wearing what item?

   A. A pair of gold glasses

   B. A mechanical hair pin

   C. A pair of inventor goggles with a purple band

   D. A bow tie made of gears

6. On one snowy evening, Journey is caught in the workshop by Edison, Jeronicus's young assistant. Together, they find what toy, designed by Journey's mother, Jessica, that Jeronicus has been struggling to bring to life?

   a. Mr. Buddy 3000

   b. The Buddy 3000

   c. Buddy 2000

   d. Buddy 2.0

7. Jeronicus's former assistant, revealed in Question #3, runs out of ideas from the book of inventions and attempts to unveil what temperamental toy of his own design?

   a. Twirly Whirly

   b. Fuzzy Buzzy

   c. Wobble Gobble

   d. Snoodle Poodle

8. As a fun nod to the multigenerational aspects of the story, at the end of the film the narrator is revealed to be which character now reading the story to their own grandchildren?

   a. Edison

   b. Jessica

   c. Journey

   d. Mrs. Johnston

ANSWERS: 1.B, 2.C, 3.D, 4.B, 5.C, 6.B, 7.A, 8.C

Secret Santa Word Search

Just like the perfect Christmas gifts under the tree, the right elements in a Christmas movie can make or break how long it stays on the yearly Christmas movie watch list. Can you match the movie to its keywords?

1. *8-Bit Christmas* (2021)
2. *Babes in Toyland* (1986)
3. *Ernest Saves Christmas* (1988)
4. *The Nutcracker* (1993)
5. *Unaccompanied Minors* (2006)

A. Orlando, Taxi, Santa
B. Nintendo, Chicago, Treehouse
C. Kingdom, Fairy, Soldiers
D. Airport, Blizzard, Canoe
E. Trollog, Toymaster, Keanu

ANSWERS: 1.B, 2.E, 3.A, 4.C, 5.D

POST-CREDITS

★ Ming Ming the elf, who tracks Buddy's progress at the North Pole and moves him to toy testing, is played by Christmas movie alum Peter Billingsley, who famously portrayed Ralphie in *A Christmas Story*.

★ *Jingle All the Way* writer Randy Kornfield was inspired to write the film after his experiences trying to track down Power Ranger toys during the shopping craze of the nineties. (I'm contractually obligated to thank my mom for getting me all these toys.)

★ EGOT winner (Emmy, Grammy, Oscar, Tony) and recording artist John Legend served as a producer on *Jingle Jangle: A Christmas Journey* and contributed songs to help fully realize a different vision of what a holiday film could be. He liked to describe it as a Black Willy Wonka set against the holidays.

6

The Naughty List

A RAUNCHY CHRISTMAS

For those of you who prefer your Santa to be dropping f-bombs instead of gifts down the chimney and think holiday spirit is 80 proof, then there's a genre of Christmas movie for you! Reveling in a perverse pleasure that defies the candy-coated conventions of yesteryear, these rude, crude, and devilishly enjoyable R-rated films let comedy reign supreme. They feature unfiltered, unabashed, and unapologetically irreverent scripts with punchlines as spicy as gingerbread.

In this universe, an office Secret Santa gift comes with antibiotics and regret the next morning; overworked moms might blow off steam by giving Kris Kringle a grown-up dance; familiar friends with a penchant for fast food reunite in 3D; two strangers from disparate walks of life exact revenge on a couple of grinches; and Santa Claus is real . . . even if he has a bad attitude. But it's okay in the end, because his heart really does grow a few sizes—and it isn't just from his high cholesterol.

A Bad Moms Christmas

Year: 2017

Directors: Scott Moore, Jon Lucas

Writers: Jon Lucas, Scott Moore

Cast: Mila Kunis, Kristen Bell, Kathryn Hahn, Cheryl Hines, Christine Baranski

Plot: In this sequel to *Bad Moms*, Amy, Kiki, and Carla, three underappreciated and overburdened moms, face an entirely new challenge for Christmas: hosting their own mothers.

1. Sandy enjoys various things: hailing from Bismarck, North Dakota; mimicking her daughter's hairstyle; and watching Kiki fall asleep. What night does Sandy not watch her daughter fall asleep?

   A. *NCIS* night

   B. *Law and Order* night

   C. *Blue Bloods* night

   D. *Suits* night

Cheer-O-Meter

Christmas Spirit

Warm Fuzzies

Timelessness

Festive Fact

Kathryn Hahn (who plays Carla) wrote a personal letter to Susan Sarandon asking her to play her mother in the film. She said, "My ovaries really need you in this movie. I feel it." Sarandon replied, "Who am I to argue with your ovaries?"

2. Carla admits to Amy and Kiki that each year for Christmas, instead of shopping, she wraps up household items and her son, Jax, is none the wiser. What gift has he received nine times?

   A. Baseball glove

   B. Basketball

   C. Soccer ball

   D. Football helmet

3. Preferring to enjoy Christmas rather than rushing around to find a tree, Amy decides to steal a tree from what store in the mall?

   A. Sephora

   B. JCPenney

   C. Lady Foot Locker

   D. Victoria's Secret

4. During the Christmas party, Ruth stresses to Amy that she can't kick what music artist and national treasure out of her house? (Amy does so anyway.)

   A. Michael Bolton

   B. Kenny G

   C. Michael Bublé

   D. Josh Groban

5. Carla introduces Kiki and Amy to Ty Swindle (who she met while waxing his jingle bells) at a Sexy Santa competition, where he dances and competes under what number?

   A. 1

   B. 2

   C. 6

   D. 9

6. To win the Caroling Cup, Amy's family must visit three hundred houses (with the help of the Chicago All Saints Choir) dressed in costume as characters from what story?

   A. *How the Grinch Stole Christmas!*

   B. *The Night Before Christmas*

   C. *The Polar Express*

   D. *A Christmas Carol*

7. All three families (and, yes, even Ruth) enjoy what kind of food for Christmas dinner?

   A. Pizza

   B. BBQ

   C. Chinese

   D. Burger King

8. Instead of saying how he feels, Ty shows Carla his true feelings by using the universal language of dance, performing in front of everyone to the tune of what Christmas song?

   A. "Santa Baby"

   B. "Back Door Santa"

   C. "All I Want for Christmas Is You"

   D. "Merry Christmas Baby"

Festive Fact

This isn't the first time that Christine Baranski (who plays Ruth) has portrayed a character obsessed with Christmas decorations. She played the apple of the Grinch's eye, Martha May Whovier, in *Dr. Seuss' How the Grinch Stole Christmas* in 2000.

Bad Santa

Year: 2003

Director: Terry Zwigoff

Writers: Glenn Ficarra, John Requa

Cast: Billy Bob Thornton, Tony Cox, Lauren Graham, Brett Kelly, Bernie Mac

Plot: A con man named Willie dresses as a mall Santa for an annual Christmas Eve heist. This twisted holiday tale delivers a sleigh full of raunchy humor and unexpected heart, making it a cult favorite for those who like Christmas with a side of cynicism.

Cheer-O-Meter

Christmas Spirit

Warm Fuzzies

Timelessness

1. Willie, a miserable con man and Santa Claus impersonator, and his friend Marcus, who poses as his elf, travel to what Southwest city for the majority of the film?

   A. Phoenix

   B. Albuquerque

   C. Tucson

   D. Santa Fe

Festive Fact

Several times throughout shooting, actor Billy Bob Thornton went a little too method with his character's love of good cheer. He indulged so much one morning that he nearly passed out on the ride up the escalator.

2. What special Christmas gift does Thurman initially ask Willie for that (one way or another, with a little blood) ends up on his doorstep on Christmas?

   A. A gorilla named Davey

   B. A purple stuffed elephant

   C. A new Advent calendar

   D. A pink stuffed elephant

3. Willie scares a collection of families at the mall by arriving at his post three sleigh bells to the wind. To the shock of onlookers, he punches the head off of what display character?

   A. Frosty the Snowman

   B. A Christmas donkey

   C. A blow-up penguin

   D. A nutcracker

4. How does Thurman explain the absence of his father to Willie?

   A. He's in jail

   B. He's on a mission from God

   C. He's exploring the mountains

   D. He's with another family

5. When security chief Gin Slagel uncovers Willie and Marcus's plan to rob Saguaro Square Mall, he wants a taste of the money. How much of a taste does Gin want?

   A. 30 percent

   B. All of it

   C. 48 percent

   D. Half

6. Remorseful after destroying Thurman's Advent calendar, Willie fixes it and fills one of the doors with what non-Christmas-y candy?

   A. Blue M&M's

   B. Candy corn

   C. Easter egg bubble gum

   D. Tic Tacs

7. A shirtless Willie and Sue (Mrs. Santa's sister) are interrupted by Thurman, who tells Willie he wanted to give him his Christmas gift early. What did he get Willie?

   A. A bottle opener

   B. A new razor

   C. A wooden pickle

   D. A pair of sandals

Festive Fact

Bill Murray was in final negotiations to star in the film but dropped out for *Lost in Translation*.

8. Thurman disposes of the head skateboarding bully with a swift kick to the silver bells. As he rides away on his two-wheeled chariot, he wears a T-shirt emblazoned with what vulgar affirmation?

   A. "Never carol on an empty stomach"

   B. "I do it for the ho ho hos"

   C. "North Pole streaking champion"

   D. "Sh*t happens when you party naked"

ANSWERS: 1.A, 2.D, 3.B, 4.C, 5.D, 6.B, 7.C, 8.D

Office Christmas Party

Year: 2016

Directors: Josh Gordon, Will Speck

Writers: Justin Malen, Laura Solon, Dan Mazer

Cast: Jason Bateman, Olivia Munn, T. J. Miller, Jennifer Aniston, Kate McKinnon

Plot: In a last-ditch effort to land a big client and save their jobs, Josh, Clay, and Tracey throw a debaucherous office Christmas party that quickly escalates into chaotic depravity.

1. **Clay (mostly Josh) runs the Chicago branch of what tech company that's at the center of the titular party?**

   A.   Zenotek

   B.   Enotech

   C.   Inotek

   D.   Cybertech

Cheer-O-Meter

Christmas Spirit

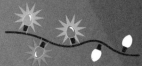

Warm Fuzzies

Timelessness

Festive Fact

While waiting in the first-class lounge at the airport and chewing out a kid, Carol (played by Jennifer Aniston) is seen holding a copy of the book *The Girl on the Train*. The film version of that book starred Justin Theroux, who Aniston was married to at the time.

2. In the hopes of impressing their potential new client, Tracey manages to get which NBA superstar (trying to expand their empire in the tech space) to attend the party?

    A. LeBron James

    B. Giannis Antetokounmpo

    C. Jimmy Butler

    D. Shaquille O'Neal

3. Despite being made out of "salad and Smartwater," Carol is highly trained in what martial art that she uses to take out some Russian thugs to everyone's surprise?

    A. Jeet Kune Do

    B. Karate

    C. Kung fu

    D. Krav Maga

4. What is the name of the miracle software developed by Tracey over the course of a few years that saves the company when the city's power is knocked out by Clay crashing a car into a building?

    A. AirConnect

    B. Anywair

    C. AnyLink

    D. AirLink

5. Clay, dressed as Santa Claus, hands out gifts (they're massagers!) to his employees at the party while sitting in what special location?

    A. Atop a live reindeer

    B. Captain Kirk's chair from *Star Trek*

    C. On the Iron Throne from *Game of Thrones*

    D. A replica of H. G. Wells's time machine

6. **In the first-class lounge at the airport, Carol pretends to call Santa to punish a little girl named Darcy for doing what to her that makes the evening that much worse?**

   A.   Taking her seat

   B.   Calling her old

   C.   Scuffing her brand-new Louboutins

   D.   Eating her Cinnabon

7. **Josh and Tracey reluctantly agree to reprise their dance performance from the previous year's party, where they dressed up as what?**

   A.   Teddy bears

   B.   Reindeer

   C.   Elves

   D.   Snowmen

8. **Onstage, Clay performs what song (with a little help from Mary) that really gets the crowd going?**

   A.   "Insane in the Brain" by Cypress Hill

   B.   "Jump Around" by House of Pain

   C.   "Just a Friend" by Biz Markie

   D.   "Let Me Clear My Throat" by DJ Kool

Festive Fact

When Josh, Tracey, and Clay go for their big pitch meeting at a hotel, the exterior of the building they enter belongs to the Civic Opera House, the second-largest opera auditorium in North America.

ANSWERS: 1.A, 2.C, 3.D, 4.B, 5.C, 6.D, 7.D, 8.D

The Night Before

Cheer-O-Meter

Christmas Spirit

Warm Fuzzies

Timelessness

Year: 2015

Director: Jonathan Levine

Writers: Jonathan Levine, Kyle Hunter, Ariel Shaffir, Evan Goldberg

Cast: Joseph Gordon-Levitt, Seth Rogen, Anthony Mackie, Lizzy Caplan, Jillian Bell

Plot: Three lifelong friends on the brink of entering adulthood embark on a decades-long quest to find the holy grail of Christmas parties in New York City.

1. **Which of these Christmas Eve traditions is not included in the boys' yearly itinerary?**
    A. Rockefeller Center Christmas Tree
    B. Hockey in Central Park
    C. Chinese food
    D. FAO Schwarz

2. **What is the name of the uber-secretive and exclusive holy grail Christmas party characterized as "so great that words cannot describe"?**
    A. Happy Holidaze
    B. The Jolly Jamboree
    C. The Nutcracker Ball
    D. ChrisMischief

3. **What thankless job did Ethan have at the beginning of the film before he quits in dramatic fashion upon finding the tickets to the elusive party he's spent ten years looking for?**

   A. Mall Santa Claus

   B. Elf waiter

   C. Reindeer pooper scooper

   D. Barista

4. **Due to a mix of substances provided by his wife, Betsy, from Craigslist, Isaac hallucinates, engages in a conversation with a statue named Spencer, and later vomits in front of Betsy's entire family where?**

   A. In a taxi

   B. At Christmas dinner

   C. At a Radio City Rockettes performance

   D. At midnight Mass

5. **Mr. Green, the trio's former high school Secret Santa (and, as it turns out, an angel who loves *The Great Gatsby*), is played by what Oscar-nominated actor known more for their dramatic roles?**

   A. Mark Ruffalo

   B. Michael Shannon

   C. Bradley Cooper

   D. Edward Norton

6. What is the name of the "nice and eloquent man" who repeatedly sends naked pictures to Sarah's phone?

   A. James

   B. Phil

   C. Zova

   D. Cho

7. Rebecca, the ill-natured superfan, acts as a general nuisance to the group and mentions that her favorite Christmas heroes include all but which of the following?

   A. Hans Gruber

   B. The Sticky Bandits

   C. Ebenezer Scrooge

   D. The Grinch

8. When Isaac's new baby won't sleep, the boys serenade her with what song that they performed at their favorite karaoke bar on Christmas Eve?

   A. "Christmas in Hollis" by Run-D.M.C.

   B. "Runaway" by Kanye West

   C. "Christmas (Baby Please Come Home)" by Darlene Love

   D. "Father Figure" by George Michael

Festive Fact

Director Jonathan Levine, reuniting with Rogen and Gordon-Levitt after 50/50, said most of the comedic portions of the film were heavily improvised and the dramatic portions stuck to the script.

Trading Places

Cheer-O-Meter

Christmas Spirit

Warm Fuzzies

Timelessness

Year: 1983

Director: John Landis

Writers: Timothy Harris, Herschel Weingrod

Cast: Eddie Murphy, Dan Aykroyd, Jamie Lee Curtis, Ralph Bellamy, Don Ameche

Plot: In this biting satire, the lives of a snobbish investor and a wily street con artist collide due to a cruel bet between two callous millionaire brothers over the age-old nature vs. nurture debate.

1. In the film's opening, set to an arrangement of Mozart's overture from *The Marriage of Figaro*, a montage showcases historical sites and locations from which city, the primary location of the film?

   A. New York City

   B. Chicago

   C. Boston

   D. Philadelphia

2. Randolph and Mortimer, the film's greedy antagonists, run what commodities brokerage firm that's at the center of the plot?

   A. Baum & Baum

   B. Smith & Smith

   C. Duke & Duke

   D. Wilson & Wilson

3. When a crooked cop (played by Frank Oz, famed Muppeteer and voice of Yoda) books Louis at the station, which of the following items is NOT confiscated?

   A. Angel dust

   B. American Express Gold Card

   C. Two tickets to *La Bohéme*

   D. Gold-plated cufflinks

Festive Fact

Prior to the film, Don Ameche (who plays Mortimer) hadn't worked for fourteen years. Just a few short years later, he would win an Oscar for Best Supporting Actor in Cocoon.

4. What is the Shakespeare-inspired name of the character played by Jamie Lee Curtis, who offers to help Louis when he's at his lowest point to secure her own retirement?

   A. Cordelia

   B. Ophelia

   C. Emilia

   D. Viola

5. Wearing a filthy Santa costume, an armed Louis crashes the holiday party in the hopes of getting his life back. What specific food item does Louis steal and later eat through his grungy beard on the bus?

   A. Turkey leg

   B. Salmon

   C. Spaghetti

   D. Steak

6. **Randolph and Mortimer settle their nature vs. nurture wager in the bathroom during the Christmas party. How much did the winner get?**

   A. $1

   B. $1,000

   C. $100,000

   D. $1,000,000

7. **Billy Ray and Louis stumble on Randolph and Mortimer's plot to profit from trades in which futures contract?**

   A. Gold

   B. Frozen concentrated orange juice

   C. Pork bellies

   D. Coffee

8. **What is security expert Clarence Beeks dressed as while he is tied up and secretly shipped out of the country?**

   A. Security guard

   B. Christmas package

   C. Antiquities box

   D. Gorilla

BANK

Festive Fact

Randolph and Mortimer make a cameo in another Eddie Murphy film, *Coming to America*, as vagrants reeling from the events of the first film. When Murphy's character, Prince Akeem, gives them a wad of cash, Randolph exclaims, "Mortimer, we're back!"

SPOTLIGHT QUIZ

A Very Harold & Kumar Christmas

Year: 2011

Director: Todd Strauss-Schulson

Writers: Jon Hurwitz, Hayden Schlossberg

Cast: Kal Penn, John Cho, Neil Patrick Harris, Patton Oswalt, Danneel Harris

A Very Harold & Kumar Christmas is the third film in the Harold & Kumar franchise and a standout addition to the raunchy holiday oeuvre thanks to its unapologetic embrace of the series's three rules according to screenwriters Jon Hurwitz and Hayden Schlossberg: there must be a certain green plant, there must be nudity, there must be Neil Patrick Harris. Add a magic gift from Santa, an all-important Christmas tree hunt, a Christmas extravaganza starring NPH, a giant killer snowman, and a snowstorm to the tune of Bing Crosby's "White Christmas," and you have one irreverent holiday comedy full of merry mischief and yuletide cheer.

Cheer-O-Meter

Christmas Spirit

Warm Fuzzies

Timelessness

Festive Fact

Neil Patrick Harris's real-life husband, David Burtka, cameos as fictional (and straight) Neil Patrick Harris's dealer and media husband in the film.

1. Neil Patrick Harris, who was eighty-sixed from Heaven, is now telepathic and gives the boys what popular toy that later saves both of their lives?

   A. WaffleBot

   B. PancakeBot

   C. TacoBot

   D. BobaBot

2. A magic gift from Santa, created to reunite Harold and Kumar, accidentally burns down what variety of Christmas tree that Maria's father, Carlos, had been growing for eight years?

   A. Balsam fir

   B. Scotch pine

   C. Fraser fir

   D. Douglas fir

3. While the boys are stranded, Harold shoots a shotgun in the air hoping to alert someone but instead shoots down what? Kumar saves the day by doing life-saving surgery.

   A. A partridge in a pear tree

   B. A hot-air balloon carrying an engaged couple

   C. Santa Claus

   D. A rare Steller's sea eagle

4. During a shootout, Harold and Kumar narrowly escape the penthouse of mobster Sergei Katsov, leaving their friends behind, and take the elevator down to the ground level. When they exit, what do they encounter?

   A. A White Castle

   B. A reindeer-themed strip club

   C. Christmas carolers

   D. They are transformed into Claymation

5. What classic Christmas movie is on the television (and referenced later in the film) when Vanessa tells Kumar she's pregnant? He says he was paying attention to her and the TV.

   A. *It's a Wonderful Life*

   B. *A Christmas Story*

   C. *Home Alone*

   D. *A Charlie Brown Christmas*

ANSWERS: 1.A, 2.C, 3.C, 4.D, 5.B

POST-CREDITS

★ ***Bad Santa*** is dedicated to actor John Ritter (who played prudish mall manager Bob Chipeska) in what would be his final live-action film before he passed in 2003.

★ Inspired by the ending of ***Trading Places***, which pointed out a loophole in the system, the Dodd-Frank Wall Street Reform and Consumer Protection Act was signed into law in 2010 and contained a provision known as the "Eddie Murphy Rule," making it illegal to use nonpublic information from government agencies to trade in the futures market.

★ Kal Penn (Kumar in ***A Very Harold & Kumar Christmas***) had to leave his position in the US Office of Public Liaison under President Obama to film this movie and return to his beloved, wisecracking character.

The Magic of Christmas

DRAMA AND FANTASY

Christmas has always been a time of year that feels magical, whether you are strolling through a twinkling town square with carolers on every corner, watching snow flurries dance under streetlights on a blisteringly cold night, or spending time with loved ones exchanging gifts and memories. But Christmas is also a time of physical magic. We're talking about magic that allows Santa to tap his nose and disappear or divine intervention in the form of Cary Grant whisking your wife away to convince you to find your faith again.

The lessons learned in each film serve as a reminder that even in the coldest and darkest times, there is always the promise of light and warmth. And although the characters in these films might need angels, magical reindeer, or talking animals with the voice of Stephen Merchant to succeed, they ultimately remind us that all we need to make our wishes come true is ourselves and a little faith. And that's the greatest Christmas gift of all. (But Cary Grant is a close second.)

A Boy Called Christmas

Year: 2021

Director: Gil Kenan

Writers: Ol Parker, Gil Kenan

Cast: Henry Lawfull, Toby Jones, Sally Hawkins, Kristen Wiig, Michiel Huisman

Plot: Nikolas embarks on a magical adventure through harsh conditions in search of his father, who is on a quest to discover a fabled land of magical elves.

Cheer-O-Meter

Christmas Spirit

Warm Fuzzies

Timelessness

1. It's present-day London, and three young children are told a story by their aunt Ruth about an ordinary boy in Finland named Nikolas (called "Christmas" by his mother), who dreams of the stories his mother told him and befriends what kind of animal that he calls Miika?

   A. Turtle

   B. Squirrel

   C. Mouse

   D. Bear

Festive Fact

The film was shot in a number of international locations, including London; the High Tatras Mountains in Slovakia; Prague, the Czech Republic; and near the arctic circle in Lapland, Finland.

2. Nikolas's father, a woodcutter named Joel, is inspired by the king to go on an expedition to the far north in search of what magical land that Nikolas's mother used to tell him about when he was a child?

   A. Eldergrove

   B. Elfhelm

   C. Elvoria

   D. Evershade

3. After Joel leaves on his quest, Nikolas is watched over by his cruel aunt Carlotta, who cooks a soup with what meaningful vegetable that his mom carved into a doll for him?

   A. Turnip

   B. Pumpkin

   C. Radish

   D. Potato

4. Nikolas leaves to find his father with Miika, who can now talk, and together they encounter a reindeer in the forest that has been shot by an arrow. What does Nikolas name this friendly reindeer?

   A. Donner

   B. Prancer

   C. Dasher

   D. Blitzen

5. On his long and winding journey, temperatures plummet and Nikolas begins to freeze but is saved by two elves named Father Topo and Little Noosh using what kind of special spell?

   A. Hope spell

   B. Revival spell

   C. Renewal spell

   D. Glimmer spell

6. When Nikolas escapes the clutches of a troll thanks to his new friend, a Truth Pixie, he finds the missing elf being held hostage by the humans, including his father. When he brings the elf back to his parents, what do they offer him in thanks?

   A. Toy lighthouses

   B. Spinning tops

   C. Rocking horses

   D. A quiver of arrows

7. On Christmas night, Nikolas, Miika, the reindeer, and the king deliver presents to happy children all over the kingdom, creating the first memories of Christmas. Despite the hardships he received from her, Nikolas even delivers what gift to Aunt Carlotta?

   A. Candy canes

   B. Chocolate

   C. Gumdrops

   D. Marshmallows

8. Back in London, Aunt Ruth finishes the story and the three children (who are mourning the loss of their mother) find a new appreciation for Christmas—and their empty house now magically decorated. Who does Aunt Ruth reveal herself to be at the end of the film?

   A. Mother Vodol

   B. Nikolas's mom

   C. The Truth Pixie

   D. Mrs. Claus

Festive Fact

The film stars three actors from the *Harry Potter* franchise: Maggie Smith (Minerva McGonagall), Jim Broadbent (Horace Slughorn), and Toby Jones (Dobby the elf).

ANSWERS: 1C, 2B, 3A, 4D, 5A, 6B, 7B, 8C

It's a Wonderful Life

Cheer-O-Meter

Christmas Spirit

Warm Fuzzies

Timelessness

Year: 1946

Director: Frank Capra

Writers: Frances Goodrich, Albert Hackett, Frank Capra, Jo Swerling

Cast: James Stewart, Donna Reed, Lionel Barrymore, Thomas Mitchell, Henry Travers

Plot: George Bailey is a man overwhelmed by life's challenges and on the brink of despair. On Christmas Eve, he finds himself on a transformative journey thanks to a guardian angel who shows him what the world would be like without him.

Festive Fact

The film was originally developed with Cary Grant as the lead until Frank Capra came aboard and retooled it for Jimmy Stewart.

1. How did George lose hearing in his left ear, resulting in him not being eligible to join the war and forever changing the course of his life?

   A. Mr. Gower angrily smacked him on the head

   B. He got frostbite while sledding without a hat

   C. An infection from saving his drowning brother

   D. He fell off his roof helping his father put up Christmas lights

THE MAGIC OF CHRISTMAS

2. George and Mary walk through moonlit Bedford Falls singing "Buffalo Gals" and throw wish rocks at what house that, one day, will become their own?

   A. Old Manville House

   B. Old Granville House

   C. Old Danville House

   D. Old Stanville House

3. Wearing the unstylish underwear that he passed away in, Clarence introduces himself to George, whom he has just saved from the freezing water. Clarence says he's an angel from Heaven with what classification?

   A. AS1

   B. AS2

   C. AS3

   D. AS4

4. What character who calls George Bailey his best friend moves out of Potter's Field to a new home in Bailey Park thanks to George and the Building and Loan?

   A. Nick

   B. Ernie

   C. Billy

   D. Mr. Martini

5. Clarence gives George a great gift: a chance to see what the world would be like without him in it. What does NOT happen in the alternative timeline where Bedford Falls becomes Pottersville?

   A. Mr. Gower spends twenty years in jail for accidental poisoning

   B. Billy is institutionalized after the Building and Loan fails

   C. George's mother dies of a broken heart

   D. Mary is a librarian who doesn't know George

6. George screams to the heavens, "I want to live again!" His wish is granted when snow begins to fall. Who is the first person George sees, and what proof does he find that he's back home?

   A. Bert / Zuzu's flower petals in his pocket

   B. Ernie / a picture of his family in his pocket

   C. Violet / his license in his pocket

   D. Billy / a Building and Loan receipt in his pocket

Festive Fact

It's a common misconception that *Sesame Street* characters Bert and Ernie were named after Bert the policeman and Ernie the cab driver. While it would be cool, it's merely a coincidence.

7. George runs through the snow-covered streets of Bedford Falls wishing merry Christmas to residents, the wonderful old Building and Loan building, and even Mr. Potter himself, who replies in what way to George?

   A. "Merry Christmas, George!"

   B. "And a happy New Year to you!"

   C. "Away! You're smudging my windows!"

   D. "And a happy New Year to you. In jail!"

8. The theme of *It's a Wonderful Life* is beautifully rendered in a gift from Clarence to George. Can you complete the message? "Dear George!—Remember _____. Thanks for the wings! Love Clarence."

   A. No man is a failure who has family

   B. No man is a failure who has friends

   C. No man is a failure who has goodwill

   D. No man is a failure who has community

Prancer

Year: 1989

Director: John Hancock

Writer: Greg Taylor

Cast: Sam Elliott, Rebecca Harrell, Cloris Leachman, Abe Vigoda, Michael Constantine

Plot: As her family's farm falls on hard times, a young girl named Jessica discovers a wounded reindeer in the forest that she believes to be Santa's very own Prancer.

Cheer-O-Meter

Christmas Spirit

Warm Fuzzies

Timelessness

1. After being told by her teacher to not sing so loud, Jessica performs in a Christmas pageant at school dressed as what character from the Nativity?

   A. An angel

   B. A shepherd

   C. Mary

   D. Innkeeper

2. Jessica's grieving father, John, is struggling and is considering sending Jessica to live with his sister-in-law. What kind of farm does John own?

   A. Pumpkin

   B. Cherry

   C. Apple

   D. Corn

3. Jessica's best friend, Carol, gets on her bad side and becomes Jessica's ex–best friend for a portion of the movie for telling her what?

    A. That Santa isn't real

    B. That Prancer isn't real

    C. That Heaven isn't real

    D. That she's on the Naughty List

4. When Prancer magically shows up on the Riggs farm, Jessica notices that he's been hurt. How exactly does Jessica lure an injured reindeer across the pond and into the shed?

    A. Apples

    B. Carrots

    C. Singing

    D. Christmas cookies

5. Jessica helps clean Mrs. McFarland's house, earning how much to buy oats for Prancer?

    A. $15

    B. $18

    C. $20

    D. $5

Festive Fact

The Riggs family farm, located in LaPorte, Indiana, where the movie was filmed, was actually director John Hancock's own childhood home and farm.

6. **Jessica befriends Mrs. McFarland over the course of the workday. She cheers her up by inspiring her to do what beloved Christmas activity that she gave up years ago?**

    A. Baking Christmas cookies

    B. Playing Christmas carols on the piano

    C. Decorating her house for Christmas

    D. Making Christmas ornaments

7. **The whole town of Three Oaks finds out about Prancer thanks to a newspaper article inspired by Jessica's Santa letter and a Polaroid of Prancer. Several townspeople show up at the Riggs farm hoping for a peek, but an angry John does what when he finds the reindeer?**

    A. Locks him in the shed

    B. Lets the kids ride him

    C. Feeds him a pie and some apples

    D. Sells him to a Christmas tree farm

8. **After John reveals Prancer in his truck, he and Jessica take him to what farm so he'll be ready at midnight for Santa to pick him up?**

    A. Antler Ridge

    B. Polar Pines

    C. Glacial Grove

    D. Silver Valley

THREE OAKS NE

Finance - Politics - Editorial - Sports - Weather - TV and radio - Horoscope - City life

Festive Fact

Movie fans are sure to recognize Jessica's friend Carol as actress Ariana Richards, who is most well known for her roles as Lex in *Jurassic Park* and Mindy in *Tremors*.

THE MAGIC OF CHRISTMAS

The Bishop's Wife

Cheer-O-Meter

Christmas Spirit

Warm Fuzzies

Timelessness

Year: 1947

Director: Henry Koster

Writers: Leonardo Bercovici, Robert E. Sherwood

Cast: Cary Grant, Loretta Young, David Niven, Monty Woolley, James Gleason

Plot: A suave and debonair angel named Dudley arrives to assist a bishop who is consumed with the ambitious task of erecting a grand cathedral. The angel ends up attending more to the bishop's neglected wife.

1. Dudley overhears Julia's troubles as she talks to Professor Wutheridge and begins to talk to the professor, jokingly arguing that they met in what city where he was teaching?

    A. Rome

    B. Paris

    C. Florence

    D. Vienna

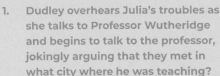

2. Henry and Julia's daughter, Debby, asks Dudley to tell her a story and to make sure it starts with "once upon a time" like a proper fairy tale. What story does he tell her?

   A. The story of Samuel

   B. The story of David

   C. The story of Isaiah

   D. The story of Daniel

3. Henry is late for a meeting at St. Timothy's because he's stuck in a meeting with Mrs. Hamilton for what reason?

   A. They're negotiating her donation

   B. He's had too much brandy

   C. He's literally stuck in a chair

   D. He's pitching her ideas for the stained-glass windows

4. Julia joins Dudley in his most wonderful evening in centuries as they ice-skate during an extended detour on their way back home. They even invite their friendly cab driver, who goes by what name, and who afterward says that his faith in humanity is restored?

   A. Sylvester

   B. Stevens

   C. Simon

   D. Sully

5. Which one of the following mini miracles does Dudley NOT perform while on his mission to help the bishop?

   A. He instantly decorates a Christmas tree

   B. He makes Professor Wutheridge's wine never empty

   C. He dictates to a typewriter that magically types

   D. He lets cars drive right through him

Festive Fact

David Niven was originally cast in the role of Dudley, with Cary Grant as the bishop. They even shot some of the film, but producer Sam Goldwyn hated what he saw and fired the director. The roles were swapped after a new director was hired.

6. Dudley helps convince Mrs. Hamilton to make a large contribution to the poor, the homeless, and the unappreciated instead of the cathedral by talking to her about what?

   A. Allan, the only love of her life

   B. Her late husband

   C. Henry and Julia's love

   D. The fact that he's an angel

7. What item of Professor Wutheridge's changes hands throughout the film and not only inspires him to continue his studies for his book but also is given as a Christmas gift to Julia at his request?

   A. His Aztec coin

   B. His Egyptian coin

   C. His Roman coin

   D. His Greek coin

8. Before Dudley departs, Henry confronts him about encroaching on his family. Henry says to Dudley, "My prayer has not been answered. I was praying for a cathedral," to which Dudley replies, "No, Henry. You were praying for _____. That has been given to you."

   A. Love

   B. Guidance

   C. Redemption

   D. Faith

Festive Fact

The young actress who plays Debby is Karolyn Grimes, who one year earlier played Zuzu Bailey in *It's a Wonderful Life* and said its most famous line.

The Family Man

Cheer-O-Meter

Christmas Spirit

Warm Fuzzies

Timelessness

Year: 2000

Director: Brett Ratner

Writers: David Diamond, David Weissman

Cast: Nicolas Cage, Téa Leoni, Jeremy Piven, Saul Rubinek, Don Cheadle

Plot: A high-flying and womanizing Wall Street executive wakes up to find his lavish lifestyle replaced by an alternate reality in which he's a suburban family man with "the one that got away."

1. It's been thirteen years since Jack left Kate at JFK Airport for an internship in London. Now, a successful Wall Street executive, he gets dressed every morning singing what song?

    A. "Lovely Day" by Bill Withers

    B. "Livin' on a Prayer" by Bon Jovi

    C. "Love Shack" by the B-52's

    D. "La donna é mobile" from *Rigoletto*

2. On Christmas Day, Jack wakes up in an alternate reality in which he's married to Kate and has two kids, a dog, and a house in the suburbs. This phenomenon isn't known as a wormhole or a different timeline, but what specific word?

    A. A glance

    B. A glimmer

    C. A glimpse

    D. A gaze

3. After Jack makes a fool of himself, Cash drives up in style in what high-end car that belongs to Jack?

   A. Ferrari

   B. Corvette

   C. Lamborghini

   D. Maserati

4. Jack's alternate-reality daughter, Annie, comes to the realization that he's not her real father and instead thinks he's what?

   A. A ghost

   B. Santa Claus

   C. An angel

   D. An alien

5. What item does Jack receive from Cash that he thinks is a special way of contacting him, when, in fact, it's just part of a Christmas present for Annie?

   A. Bicycle bell

   B. Sleigh bells

   C. Slide whistle

   D. Snow globe

6. Jack finds himself working with Kate's father, Big Ed, selling what item?

   A. Cars

   B. Tires

   C. Shoes

   D. Suits

7. Back in his reality, Jack finds photo-booth pictures used as a bookmark in what book?

   A. *A Clockwork Orange* by Anthony Burgess

   B. *The Catcher in the Rye* by J. D. Salinger

   C. *The Giver* by Lois Lowry

   D. *Cat's Cradle* by Kurt Vonnegut

8. Jack pours his heart out to Kate, and talks about all but which of the following details?

   A. Jack loves his job and is content making just enough

   B. Annie isn't much of a violin player, but she tries real hard

   C. Josh doesn't say much, but he always has his eyes open, watching

   D. Kate is a nonprofit lawyer, and it doesn't bother her

JINGLE BELL BONUS

A Little Christmas Magic

Magic always seems more magical during the Christmas season. From flying reindeer to life lessons learned in a festive time loop, the holidays are the perfect time for enchanting intervention. Can you match the movie with the source of magic within the story?

1. *Jack Frost* (1998)
2. *Last Train to Christmas* (2021)
3. *One Magic Christmas* (1985)
4. *The Chronicles of Narnia: The Lion, The Witch, and the Wardrobe* (2005)
5. *The Nutcracker and the Four Realms* (2018)

A. An angel named Gideon sent by Santa Claus

B. An armoire in the English countryside

C. A magic harmonica

D. A hallway turned tree trunk turned portal (and a mother's affirmation)

E. The 3:17 to Nottingham

ANSWERS: 1.C, 2.E, 3.A, 4.B, 5.D

POST-CREDITS

★ Six different reindeer (and a mechanical puppet) were used in the film ***Prancer***, and the main one used for the titular hero was a pregnant reindeer named Boo, hired because pregnant reindeer keep their antlers for longer, which helped the production schedule.

★ ***It's a Wonderful Life*** is based on a short story titled "The Greatest Gift" by Philip Van Doren Stern. Initially, Stern couldn't find a publisher, so he turned it into a twenty-one-page Christmas card that he sent to two hundred friends. An RKO producer saw it, and the rest is history.

★ George Clooney, Kevin Kline, and John Travolta were all considered for the part of Jack in ***The Family Man***, but writers David Diamond and David Weissman always wanted Nicolas Cage and even wrote the script with his voice in their heads.

Stocking Stuffer

Unconventional Christmas Movies

What are unconventional Christmas movies? Simply put, they're a unique niche of films straying from the typical sleigh bells and snowflakes and offering but a whisper of Christmas. From war movies to erotic thrillers, crime capers to book adaptations, these underrated or unusual films all share a common thread—a nod to Christmas woven seamlessly into their storylines without ever treading into the territory of the North Pole, elves, or magic.

2046 (2004)

Directed by visionary Hong Kong filmmaker Wong Kar-wai, this spiritual sequel to *In the Mood for Love* features a Christmas Eve scene between Chow Mo-wan and Bai Ling to the tune of a Christmas song by what unforgettable American jazz and pop vocalist?

A Midnight Clear (1992)

Father greets German soldiers by their makeshift Christmas tree and politely declines what unconventional Christmas gift, or *weihnachtsgeschenk*, from a soldier? Instead, Father gives him one of his grenades to use as a Christmas ornament.

Carol (2015)

During a magnetic meet-cute at Frankenberg's department store between housewife Carol and shopgirl Therese, what Christmas gift (at Therese's recommendation) is ultimately chosen for Carol's daughter instead a new doll?

Catch Me If You Can (2002)

On Christmas Eve (a recurring date/theme in the film), Frank calls Carl at the office and the men trade verbal jabs while clearly alone in more ways than one. At this point in the story, Frank is using what secret identity of a speedy superhero as his alias?

Edward Scissorhands (1990)

On Christmas, Kim dances under falling snow (a first in her town) made of ice flying through the air thanks to Edward's carving of an ice sculpture of what design?

Eyes Wide Shut (1999)

In Stanley Kubrick's final film, Bill must give what secret password (that shares a name with Beethoven's only opera and translates from the Latin to "faithful") to gain entry to an exclusive and debaucherous masked ball?

In Bruges (2008)

What "inanimate festive object" does Harry destroy after a call with Ken, before then calling his wife an "inanimate festive object" when she tells him to relax? (For the sake of the holiday, "festive" is replacing a word deserving of a sock full of coal.)

Little Women (1994)

Mr. Laurence (with help from the March family) surprises a severely weakened Beth on Christmas with the gift of his daughter's piano. After encouragement from Amy, what Christmas carol does Beth play?

Tangerine (2015)

At a club on Christmas Eve, Alexandra sings a haunting version of what song that first appeared in a 1903 operetta, was featured in a Laurel and Hardy Christmas movie and a 1961 Disney musical, and was covered by Doris Day for her Christmas album?

The Lion in Winter (1968)

Katharine Hepburn won her third of four Best Actress Oscars for playing estranged Queen Eleanor of Aquitaine at King Henry II's medieval Christmas party. She famously tied with what Funny Girl, who won her first and only statuette for acting?

ANSWERS: 1. Nat King Cole, 2. A gun, 3. A train set, 4. Barry Allen (The Flash), 5. Angel, 6. Fidelio, 7. A telephone, 8. "Deck the Halls," 9. "Toyland," 10. Barbra Streisand

A Timeless Christmas

THE CLASSICS

*C*lassic Christmas movies (released before 1960 for the purposes of this chapter) are known for their timeless charm and nostalgic allure. They transport viewers to a bygone era of simplicity and classic storytelling and have inspired countless modern Christmas classics. They're referenced constantly for their contributions to film history, and in one very special case, thanks to Judy Garland's memorable performance, gave birth to one of the greatest Christmas songs of all time. There really is no better subgenre of Christmas movies to watch on a snowy day in December, especially if you need a nostalgia IV straight into your veins. But what else do they offer? Elegant wardrobes, divine hairstyles, and, of course, how could we forget that amalgam of American and British pronunciation known as the transatlantic accent. Where did it go, and can we bring it back?

The early days of cinema depict a simpler time. No cell phones or Internet, no forced human interaction, and Christmas decorations that were extremely flammable—but boy did they look fantastic. What designates a movie as a classic isn't the stars or the number of awards it won, but whether its story remains relevant years later.

Christmas in Connecticut

Year: 1945

Director: Peter Godrey

Writers: Lionel Houser, Adele Comandini

Cast: Barbara Stanwyck, Dennis Morgan, Sydney Greenstreet, Reginald Gardiner, S. Z. Sakall

Plot: A popular magazine columnist renowned for her exquisite homemaking skills faces a comedic predicament when her publisher invites a war hero to her countryside home for a traditional family Christmas. The catch? It's all an elaborate ruse.

Cheer-O-Meter

Christmas Spirit

Warm Fuzzies

Timelessness

1. Written from her tiny NYC apartment, Elizabeth Lane's "Diary of a Housewife" is a column about her idyllic life in the countryside as a wife, mother, and "America's Best Cook" (all of which she's not) for what popular magazine?

    A. *Good Housekeeping*

    B. *Smart Housekeeping*

    C. *American Housekeeping*

    D. *Ladies' Home Journal*

Festive Fact

Barbara Stanwyck's gowns were designed by one of the most influential costume designers in film history, Edith Head. For modern audiences, she was one of the inspirations for Edna Mode in *The Incredibles*.

2. Finish the quote by Elizabeth: "When you're kissing me, don't talk about _____."

   A. Architecture

   B. Fireplaces

   C. Elevators

   D. Plumbing

3. Felix's favorite catchphrase is what malapropism for "everything is fine," which, depending on how he says it in his accent, can sound like two different things?

   A. Hunky Dunky

   B. Easy Peachy

   C. Peachy Kleen

   D. Cake Piece

4. In one of her columns, Elizabeth mentions she is looking for what perfect item, inspiring readers to send her thirty-eight of them—well, thirty-nine, when Jones shows up with one in Connecticut as a present?

   A. Mink coat

   B. Coffee maker

   C. Rocking chair

   D. Vacuum

5. Felix calls Norah's kitchen, purportedly the finest in Connecticut, a "catastrophe." When he smells Norah's Irish stew, he fixes it by adding what ingredient to make it a proper goulash?

   A. Paprika

   B. Garlic

   C. Worcestershire sauce

   D. Cumin

6. **Jones and Elizabeth have a romantic walk through the farm while tending to a cow with what name?**

A. Marmalade

B. Mistletoe

C. Macushla

D. Mr. Mo

7. **On Christmas Eve, Elizabeth decorates the tree as Jones plays the piano and sings "O Little Town of Bethlehem" followed by what romantic song?**

A. "The Wish That I Wish Tonight" by Ray Noble and His Orchestra

B. "She Broke My Heart in Three Places" by the Hoosier Hot Shots

C. "I Get a Kick Out of You" by Frank Sinatra

D. "A Certain Smile" by Johnny Mathis

8. **After dancing together at the town hall, Elizabeth and Jones spend the night in jail after being caught by police doing what?**

A. Canoodling in someone's barn

B. Stealing someone's bicycle

C. Sitting in a police car

D. Riding a runaway sleigh

ANSWERS: 1.B, 2.D, 3.A, 4.C, 5.A, 6.C, 7.A, 8.D

It Happened on Fifth Avenue

Year: 1947

Director: Roy Del Ruth

Writer: Everett Freeman (story by Herbert Clyde Lewis and Frederick Stephani)

Cast: Don DeFore, Ann Harding, Charles Ruggles, Victor Moore, Gale Storm

Plot: Every winter, a kindhearted hobo secretly moves into a vacated Fifth Avenue mansion for the holidays. The situation turns delightfully complex when a homeless veteran and the mansion owner's daughter also take shelter there and fall in love.

Cheer-O-Meter

Christmas Spirit

Warm Fuzzies

Timelessness

1. The action primarily takes place in a Fifth Avenue mansion that is boarded up and vacated every winter belonging to industrial wizard Michael J. O'Connor, who, according to passing bus tours, is how rich?

   A. The richest man in the world

   B. The second-richest man in the world

   C. The third-richest man in the world

   D. One of the richest men in the world

2. Living in the Fifth Avenue mansion for the past three winters is McKeever, a hobo, and his dog, Sam. What is McKeever's first name?

   A. Aloysius

   B. Ambrose

   C. Algernon

   D. Alphonse

3. McKeever and new resident Jim Bullock find O'Connor's eighteen-year-old runaway daughter, Trudy, rifling through her own closet and attempting to "steal" what item?

   A. A Dior "Chérie" dress

   B. A suitcase

   C. A mink coat

   D. A cloche hat

4. Jim, Whitey, and Hank (inspired by McKeever) decide that they are going to transform what property into affordable housing?

   A. Vacant warehouse

   B. Vacant gas station

   C. Vacant school

   D. Vacant Army barracks

5. To get Jim away from his impressionable daughter, O'Connor convinces his cronies to offer Jim a job for only single men in what South American country?

   A. Chile

   B. Bolivia

   C. Brazil

   D. Paraguay

Festive Fact

Planned to be the first movie by Liberty Films, a production company formed by Frank Capra and Samuel J. Briskin and later joined by George Stevens and William Wyler, this film had Capra slated to direct. That is, until he was sent a different script that he decided to make instead: *It's a Wonderful Life*.

6. **What character dresses up as Santa Claus during the Christmas party?**
   - A. Jim
   - B. Whitey
   - C. McKeever
   - D. O'Connor

7. **Mary, O'Connor's wife and Trudy's mother, makes what dish that delights the guests in the mansion but, most notably, her husband, who remembers why he married her?**
   - A. Minestrone soup
   - B. Breaded pork tenderloin
   - C. Slumgullion
   - D. Potato casserole

8. **Finish the quote spoken by McKeever during the final dinner in the house on New Year's Eve: "Tonight is our last night together. Our paths may never cross again. And I would like to feel that you're all my friends. For to be without friends is a serious form of _____."**
   - A. Disappointment
   - B. Loneliness
   - C. Poverty
   - D. Desolation

Meet Me in St. Louis

Cheer-O-Meter

Christmas Spirit

Warm Fuzzies

Timelessness

Year: 1944

Director: Vincente Minnelli

Writers: Irving Brecher, Fred F. Finklehoffe
(based on the novel by Sally Benson)

Cast: Judy Garland, Margaret O'Brien, Mary Astor,
Lucille Bremer, Tom Drake

Plot: This MGM romantic musical comedy is told
in a series of vignettes and set over a year in the life
of the Smith family, culminating with an unforgettable Christmas.

1. The backdrop of the film is St. Louis, Missouri, with the film taking
    place in the year leading up to what big event?

    A. Bicentennial

    B. Century of Progress

    C. The World's Fair

    D. The Olympics

2. Can you put Alonzo and Anna's four daughters in order from oldest to youngest?

    A. Tootie

    B. Esther

    C. Rose

    D. Agnes

3. What is the name of Esther's perfume, which she saves for
    special occasions only? Just don't tell her it's the same one your
    grandmother uses.

    A. Essence of Lavender

    B. Essence of Rose

    C. Essence of Vanilla

    D. Essence of Violet

4. During Halloween, dressed as
    a Horrible Ghost and a Terrible
    Drunken Ghost, Tootie and
    Agnes are told to do what when
    neighbors answer the door?

    A. Say "trick or treat"

    B. Throw flour at them

    C. Scare them

    D. Say "Happy Halloween"

Festive Fact

The inspiration for "The Trolley Song"
came from a book about old St.
Louis that Ralph Blane, cowriter of
the song, found at the Beverly Hills
Public Library. Under a picture of a
1903 trolley was the caption "Clang,
Clang, Clang, Went the Trolley."
Blane and Hugh Martin wrote the
song in about ten minutes.

5. John tells Esther that he can't take her to the Christmas ball
    because he couldn't pick up his tuxedo. Esther, noticeably upset,
    responds that she doesn't hate John, she just hates what?

    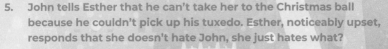

    A. The tailor

    B. St. Louis

    C. Basketball

    D. Formal dance attire

6. With love seemingly in the crisp St. Louis air, which of
    the following characters does NOT get engaged on or
    before Christmas?

    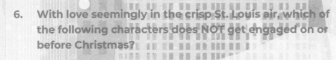

    A. Esther

    B. Warren

    C. John

    D. Lucille

7. What now-famous Christmas song (which was written for this film) does Esther sing alongside Tootie's music box as they gaze out the window?

   A. "Have Yourself a Merry Little Christmas"

   B. "I'll Be Home for Christmas"

   C. "The Christmas Song (Merry Christmas to You)"

   D. "Silent Night"

8. In the final scene, the entire family gathers at the pavilion overlooking the Grand Lagoon and is amazed at the light display. What are the final five words of the film, spoken by Esther?

   A. "You can't beat St. Louis"

   B. "Right here in St. Louis"

   C. "Let's never leave St. Louis"

   D. "St. Louis has my heart"

Festive Fact

The screenplay is based on writer Sally Benson's book of the same name, which was first published as a series of short vignettes in the *The New Yorker* titled "5135 Kensington," the address of the Smith family house.

ANSWERS: 1.C, 2.C-B-D-A, 3.D, 4.B, 5.C, 6.D, 7.A, 8.B

The Shop Around the Corner

Year: 1940

Director: Ernst Lubitsch

Writer: Samson Raphaelson

Cast: Margaret Sullavan, James Stewart, Frank Morgan, Joseph Schildkraut, Sara Haden

Plot: In a classic tale of opposites attract, two acrimonious employees of a quaint leather-goods store are blissfully unaware they're each other's beloved pen pals.

Cheer-O-Meter

Christmas Spirit

Warm Fuzzies

Timelessness

1. Adapted from Miklós László's play *Parfumerie*, this movie has seen numerous remakes. Which of the following titles is NOT a remake of *The Shop Around the Corner*?

   A. *You've Got Mail* (film)

   B. *She Loves Me* (Broadway musical)

   C. *Meet John Doe* (film)

   D. *In the Good Old Summertime* (movie musical)

2. The titular leather-goods store that's situated around the corner is located in what city?

   A. Budapest, Hungary

   B. London, England

   C. New York, New York

   D. Munich, Germany

3. Hugo, the owner of Matuschek and Company, likes to pull his employees aside and ask them what?

   A. Food recommendations

   B. Their honest opinion

   C. Relationship advice

   D. To work overtime

4. When Klara tries to get a job at Matuschek and Company, Alfred tells her none are available. She's ultimately hired after selling an undesirable musical cigarette box that plays what grating song?

   A. "La vie en rose"

   B. "Ochi Chërnye"

   C. "Funiculì, Funiculà"

   D. "Flor gitana"

5. Pirovitch intently listens as Alfred reads this excerpt from one of his anonymous letters: "My heart was trembling as I walked into the post office and there you were, lying in box _____." In what mail slot does Klara receive her letters from Alfred?

   A. 207

   B. 217

   C. 237

   D. 247

Festive Fact

Mr. Matuschek is played by actor Frank Morgan, who, one year earlier, played multiple parts including the titular character in another classic, *The Wizard of Oz*

6. While waiting for her mysterious pen pal, Klara is at the coffee shop with what kind of flower inside what famous piece of literature?

   A. Rose / *Pride and Prejudice*

   B. Carnation / *Anna Karenina*

   C. Sunflower / *Madame Bovary*

   D. Orchid / *Jane Eyre*

7. When Alfred becomes the new manager of the store, Klara has what strong reaction to hearing the news?

   A. She quits

   B. She protests

   C. She asks for a raise

   D. She faints

8. Before Alfred reveals his true identity to Klara, he plays a trick on her by saying he's met her mystery man. On top of listing some undesirable qualities, he reveals the man's name to be what?

   A. Maximus Poole

   B. Matthias Hockley

   C. Mathias Popkin

   D. Nathaniel Popham

Festive Fact

According to Jimmy Stewart biographer Roy Pickard, the café scene between Stewart and Sullavan required Stewart to do the most takes he ever did in all his movies. Forty-eight, to be exact.

ANSWERS: 1. C, 2. A, 3. B, 4. B, 5. C, 6. B, 7. D, 8. C

White Christmas

Year: 1954

Director: Michael Curtiz

Writers: Norman Krasna, Norman Panama, Melvin Frank

Cast: Bing Crosby, Danny Kaye, Rosemary Clooney, Vera-Ellen, Dean Jagger

Plot: After serving in World War II, a tandem of talented song-and-dance men team up with a sister act to save their former commanding officer's failing Vermont Inn with a lavish Christmas show.

Cheer-O-Meter

Christmas Spirit

Warm Fuzzies

Timelessness

1. What is the army division that simply loves Major General Waverly and will "follow the old man wherever he wants to go"?

   A. 801st

   B. 106th

   C. 22nd

   D. 151st

2. Ben "Freckle Faced" Haynes invites Bob and Phil to view his sister act at what Florida nightclub?

   A. Marelli's

   B. Novello's

   C. Allegro's

   D. Vittorio's

3. How does Doris respond when Bob greets her with a simple "How do you do?"

A. "Kiss my foot."

B. "Have an apple."

C. "Mutual, I'm sure."

D. "I'm a Libra."

4. In which city and state is the Columbia Inn located?

A. Maple Grove, Vermont

B. Cedar Creek, Vermont

C. Pine Tree, Vermont

D. Snow Falls, Vermont

5. When Bob is worried and can't get to sleep, he counts what?

A. Curly heads

B. Blessings

C. Clouds

D. Chickens

6. Over the course of the film, why is Major General Waverly in such a foul mood?

A. He's dying

B. The inn was bought out

C. His request to rejoin the army was denied

D. Susan, his granddaughter, is angry with him

7. During the final performance of "White Christmas" for Major General Waverly, Bob sneaks behind the Christmas tree and opens what thoughtful gift from Betty that all but solidifies their engagement?

A. A knight on a white horse

B. Her large, feathered fan

C. An overcoat and vest

D. A turtle dove ornament

8. With estimated sales in excess of fifty million copies worldwide, "White Christmas" is not only the bestselling Christmas song of all time but also the bestselling single of all time. Despite this movie's title, the song actually made its silver-screen debut a decade earlier in what other Christmas film?

A. *It's a Wonderful Life*

B. *Holiday Inn*

C. *Miracle on 34th Street*

D. *Going My Way*

ANSWERS: 1.D, 2.B, 3.C, 4.C, 5.B, 6.C, 7.A, 8.B

Guess Who's Coming to Christmas Dinner?

The Christmas dinner guest list is as important a document as anything Indiana Jones ever found in a crypt full of dust and creepy crawlers. Can you match the dinner guests (actors) with the correct dining room table (movie title)?

1. *Going My Way* (1944) / *The Bells of St. Mary's* (1945)

2. *Desk Set* (1957)

3. *Holiday Affair* (1949)

4. *Remember the Night* (1940)

5. *The Man Who Came to Dinner* (1942)

A. Janet Leigh, Robert Mitchum, Wendell Corey, Gordon Gebert

B. Bing Crosby, Barry Fitzgerald, Ingrid Bergman, Henry Travers

C. Bette Davis, Ann Sheridan, Monty Woolley, Richard Travis

D. Spencer Tracy, Katharine Hepburn, Gig Young, Joan Blondell

E. Barbara Stanwyck, Fred MacMurray, Elizabeth Patterson, Sterling Holloway

ANSWERS: 1.B, 2.D, 3.A, 4.E, 5.C

POST-CREDITS

★ ***Christmas in Connecticut*** was remade into a 1992 television film starring Kris Kristofferson, Dyan Cannon, and Tony Curtis, but the real star was the person in the director's chair: Arnold Schwarzenegger. The film was his first and most likely last foray into directing.

★ Judy Garland and director Vincente Minnelli met on **Meet Me in St. Louis** and married soon afterward. They collaborated three more times after the film with 1945's *The Clock,* 1948's *The Pirate,* and most importantly, with the birth of their daughter, Liza Minnelli, who was born in March 1946 and became a star in her own right.

★ When Bob and Phil do their version of "Sisters" in **White Christmas** to buy Betty and Judy time, Bing Crosby is genuinely cracking up at Danny Kaye's antics. Crosby assumed his laughter would disqualify the take, but after test screenings, everyone loved it and it stayed in.

9

Under the Mistletoe

ROMANCE

Aptly coined the Most Wonderful Time of the Year, the Christmas season always brings an unmatched level of romance that even the Scroogiest of singles can agree upon. Traditional dates from the previous eleven months are now transformed into holding hands while ice skating (with your hero saving you from a fall to the ice), decorating trees or freshly baked cookies (while stealing kisses on frosting-covered lips), or simply gazing into each other's eyes in front of a crackling fireplace with Bing on the radio.

At Christmas, anything seems possible! Like opening your front door to find a freezing Jude Law looking dashingly delectable on your porch. Okay, maybe that's just reserved for the movies, but it proves that there's no better genre of romance to watch on-screen than a Christmas romance. These films, and their whimsical scenarios, show us that romance during the holidays isn't about what love should be but about the beautiful possibilities of what love can be.

Last Holiday

Year: 2006

Director: Wayne Wang

Writers: Jeffrey Price, Peter S. Seaman

Cast: Queen Latifah, LL Cool J, Timothy Hutton, Gérard Depardieu, Alicia Witt

Plot: Georgia, a shy department-store saleswoman, is diagnosed with a terminal illness and cashes out her life savings to pursue the perfect final Christmas, indulging in all the pleasures she's denied herself for so long.

Cheer-O-Meter

Christmas Spirit

Warm Fuzzies

Timelessness

1. **Georgia's favorite pastime is cooking meals she never eats while watching what celebrity chef and restaurateur, who makes a surprise appearance at the end of the film?**

   A. Gordon Ramsay

   B. Wolfgang Puck

   C. Bobby Flay

   D. Emeril Lagasse

Festive Fact

Lampington's disease is a fictional disorder first created for the original version of this film, 1950's *Last Holiday*.

2. What word adorns the cover of Georgia's scrapbook, which features dreams, recipes, and, as her secret work crush Sean finds out, pictures of them in wedding attire?

   A. Possibilities

   B. Aspirations

   C. Manifestation

   D. Ambitions

3. After a knock on the head sends her to the hospital, Georgia is informed she has a rare disorder called Lampington's disease and is told she has only how long to live?

   A. Two weeks

   B. Three weeks

   C. One month

   D. Two months

4. What famous R&B singer is featured in the film during a concert at the hotel?

   A. Lionel Ritchie

   B. Smokey Robinson

   C. Luther Vandross

   D. Stevie Wonder

5. What is the name of the swanky hotel that Georgia visits in the Czech Republic?

   A. Grandhotel Pupp

   B. Le Grand Hotel

   C. Grand Hotel Czechia

   D. Resort de Las Dieux

Festive Fact

All the dishes in *Last Holiday* were prepared by chefs from the Food Network who traveled with the production.

6. What initially prevents Sean from professing his love for Georgia on New Year's Eve?

   A. Flight delay

   B. Taxi breaks down

   C. Stomach flu

   D. Avalanche

7. What is the name of the young, hip, rich, and arrogant self-help guru who not only serves as a foil to Georgia but is also the owner of the department store where she works?

   A. Matthew Keoghan

   B. Matthew Kragen

   C. Matthew Keegan

   D. Matthew Kraven

8. What feature of the hotel does Georgia comment on to the receptionist, who, later in the film, cries at how beautiful it is?

   A. The chandelier

   B. The ceiling

   C. The architecture

   D. The golden sculptures

ANSWERS: 1.D, 2.A, 3.B, 4.B, 5.A, 6.D, 7.B, 8.B

Love Actually

Year: 2003

Director: Richard Curtis

Writer: Richard Curtis

Cast: Hugh Grant, Colin Firth, Liam Neeson, Laura Linney, Emma Thompson

Plot: Romantic comedy legend Richard Curtis (*Notting Hill*, *Bridget Jones's Diary*, *Four Weddings and a Funeral*) weaves together interconnected stories about the complexities of love, in all its forms, in the weeks leading up to Christmas. These heartwarming and humorous stories, told by a star-studded cast, deliver a poignant reminder that love actually is all around.

Cheer-O-Meter

Christmas Spirit

Warm Fuzzies

Timelessness

1. A title in the beginning of the film tells us that it's how long before Christmas?

   A. One month

   B. Forty-two days

   C. Five weeks

   D. Three weeks

Festive Fact

Rufus, played by Rowan Atkinson, was originally written as an angel who overwrapped Harry's gift to prevent him from making a big mistake. You might also recall him helping Sam slip through airport security. In the final film, he's just a very helpful employee/traveler.

2. Karen's daughter, Daisy, joins a whale, an octopus, and a child with Spider-man face paint (son of writer/director Richard Curtis) on stage for the nativity play dressed as what unconventional attendee?

   A. Second Sheep

   B. First Lobster

   C. The Innkeeper's Niece

   D. Door Holder #3

3. While going door-to-door looking for Natalie in the dodgy end of Wandsworth, David is asked by three young children to sing a Christmas carol. Aided by his vocally gifted copper, Gavin, what do they sing?

   A. "We Three Kings"

   B. "Jingle Bells"

   C. "Deck the Halls"

   D. "Good King Wenceslas"

4. In the Robert Palmer–inspired music video for "Christmas Is All Around" (itself a cover of the Troggs' "Love Is All Around"), Billy Mack's backing band is composed of leggy lipsticked models wearing what?

   A. Sexy Santa costumes

   B. Sexy elf costumes

   C. Sexy reindeer costumes

   D. Sexy snowman costumes

5. Which of the following materials does Rufus NOT use when gift wrapping in the flashiest of flashes?

   A. Flower buds

   B. Cinnamon sticks

   C. Holly

   D. Red ribbon

6. Daniel repeatedly mentions that the only other woman he could possibly love is what supermodel, who, in a Christmas miracle, makes a cameo in the film as Carol, the mother of Sam's classmate?

    A. Cindy Crawford

    B. Claudia Schiffer

    C. Christie Brinkley

    D. Elle Macpherson

7. After their work Christmas party, Sarah and Karl's hopes for a romantic rendezvous are dashed by Sarah's brother, who, in a frustrating moment for superfans, calls her requesting that she get who on the phone?

    A. Elton John

    B. The Prime Minister

    C. The Pope

    D. Paul Hollywood

8. Harry gives Karen what "surprise" gift the night before Christmas that eventually brings her to tears in their bedroom?

    A. Gold-plated heart necklace

    B. A Tori Amos vinyl

    C. Cashmere gloves

    D. A Joni Mitchell CD

Love Hard

Year: 2021

Director: Hernán Jiménez

Writers: Danny Mackey, Rebecca Ewing

Cast: Nina Dobrev, Jimmy O. Yang, Darren Barnet, James Saito, Harry Shum Jr.

Plot: An LA dating columnist finds her perfect match on a dating app and impulsively buys a plane ticket to fly thousands of miles away to surprise him for Christmas. When she arrives at his doorstep, she realizes she's been catfished.

Cheer-O-Meter

Christmas Spirit

Warm Fuzzies

Timelessness

1. **What is the name of the dating app that first brings Natalie and Josh together?**

   A. Bumble

   B. SwaGr

   C. Tinder

   D. Flirt Alert

2. **What Christmas song (which Natalie hates with a passion) does Josh rewrite on the spot while they reluctantly carol in front of the nursing home?**

   A. "Santa Baby"

   B. "Mistress for Christmas"

   C. "Baby, It's Cold Outside"

   D. "Santa Tell Me"

Festive Fact

Like Josh does in the film, John Legend and Kelly Clarkson famously updated the lyrics of this classic to address potential concerns around content deemed offensive through a modern lens. This moment is a nice nod by filmmakers to highlight the changing times.

3. In the first instance of doubting her attraction to Tag, Natalie recoils after learning that Tag's favorite author is what famously reclusive American writer?

A. Herman Melville

B. Henry David Thoreau

C. Ernest Hemingway

D. John Updike

4. The film's finale features a reference to arguably the most famous scene from what Christmas movie that Natalie and Josh disagree on being the best Christmas movie ever?

A. *Love Actually*

B. *It's a Wonderful Life*

C. *White Christmas*

D. *A Christmas Story*

5. What is Natalie's favorite childhood book?

A. *Charlotte's Web*

B. *A Light in the Attic*

C. *Where the Wild Things Are*

D. *Where the Sidewalk Ends*

6. Josh uses the Simple Minds song "Don't You (Forget About Me)" to help calm Natalie while she nervously partakes in what activity?

   A. Bobsledding

   B. Rock climbing

   C. Ice skating

   D. Skydiving

7. What is the name of the store Josh's family owns and operates?

   A. Outdoor World

   B. Nature's Playground

   C. All Things Outdoors

   D. Adventure Outfitters

8. At the end of the film, Josh is relieved to learn that his father supports his secret dream of running a business making what?

   A. Snow globes

   B. Masculine candles

   C. Hand-knit Christmas sweaters

   D. Flavored marshmallows

Festive Fact

Next to the rock-climbing wall at Josh's family store, a small plaque reads: "Great things are done by a series of small things brought together." This is a quote from Vincent van Gogh.

ANSWERS: 1.D, 2.C, 3.B, 4.A, 5.D, 6.B, 7.C, 8.B

The Holiday

Year: 2006

Director: Nancy Meyers

Writer: Nancy Meyers

Cast: Cameron Diaz, Kate Winslet, Jude Law, Jack Black, Eli Wallach

Plot: Two women, Amanda from Los Angeles and Iris from England, meet online and decide to swap their homes for the holiday season to escape their respective romantic troubles. As they navigate their new surroundings, Iris and Amanda embrace the power of the holiday season.

Cheer-O-Meter

Christmas Spirit

Warm Fuzzies

Timelessness

1. **What is the name of the quaint and cozy cottage in Surrey where Iris lives and Amanda vacations?**

   A. Mill House

   B. Rosehill

   C. Meadow View

   D. Danemead

2. **Amanda is working on a trailer for an action film releasing on Christmas Day that stars James Franco and Lindsay Lohan with what one-word title?**

   A. *Retribution*

   B. *Vital*

   C. *Payback*

   D. *Deception*

3. Proud of herself after finally standing up to Jasper, Iris likes to think she has what quality shared by actress Irene Dunne and Arthur's late wife?

   A. Gumption

   B. Moxie

   C. Pizzazz

   D. Spunk

4. At Blockbuster, Miles plays a musical game performing famous movie scores (as only Jack Black can) to the delight of Iris. Which of these films does he NOT perform?

   A. *Chariots of Fire*

   B. *Driving Miss Daisy*

   C. *The Mission*

   D. *Gone with the Wind*

5. Over the course of her holiday, Amanda learns that Graham is many things: a book editor, a widower, and the alter ego of what spoon-smoking character beloved by his children?

   A. Dr. Napkin Head

   B. Napkin Head

   C. Mr. Napkin Head

   D. Sir Napkin Head

6. Amanda finally lets loose by drunkenly dancing and singing to what song?

   A. "Are You Gonna Be My Girl" by Jet

   B. "Rockin' around the Christmas Tree" by Brenda Lee

   C. "You Send Me" by Aretha Franklin

   D. "Mr. Brightside" by The Killers

7. Arthur tells Iris that, in the movies, there are two types of ladies: one that she is and one that she's behaving like. Can you name them both?

   A. The leading lady / the best friend

   B. The starlet / the comic relief

   C. The ingenue / the best friend

   D. The leading lady / the other woman

8. Arthur added one word to a famous line of dialogue from what classic Hollywood film?

   A. *It's a Wonderful Life*

   B. *The Philadelphia Story*

   C. *His Girl Friday*

   D. *Casablanca*

While You Were Sleeping

Year: 1995

Director: Jon Turteltaub

Writers: Daniel G. Sullivan, Fredric Lebow

Cast: Sandra Bullock, Bill Pullman, Peter Gallagher, Peter Boyle, Jack Warden

Plot: On Christmas, Lucy, a lonely token collector, rescues Peter, who has fallen onto the train tracks. At the hospital, Peter is in a coma and his family mistakes Lucy for his fiancée.

Cheer-O-Meter

Christmas Spirit

Warm Fuzzies

Timelessness

1. While trying to pull a Christmas tree up the side of her apartment, Lucy tells her cat that she should have bought what variety of tree because it's lighter?

   A. Fraser fir

   B. Balsam fir

   C. Blue spruce

   D. White pine

Festive Fact

The Chicago Transit Authority granted the film special access, the first time it had done that for a movie.

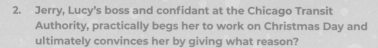

2. Jerry, Lucy's boss and confidant at the Chicago Transit Authority, practically begs her to work on Christmas Day and ultimately convinces her by giving what reason?

   A. She has no family

   B. She's single

   C. She's out of overtime

   D. It's a family emergency

3. When he's not bragging about inventing aluminum foil, Joe Fusco Jr. is relentless in asking out Lucy. He even knows a guy who can get tickets to what event?

   A. The Bulls game

   B. *Guys and Dolls*

   C. The Art Institute

   D. Ice Capades

4. Where do Jack and Lucy share their first kiss?

   A. In Peter's apartment

   B. Under the mistletoe

   C. On a patch of ice where they've fallen

   D. Next to Peter's hospital bed

5. During the epilogue, Lucy mentions that Peter asked her when she fell in love with Jack. Her response?

   A. "When he gave me the rocking chair."

   B. "On Christmas Day."

   C. "While you were sleeping."

   D. "When you were in a coma."

6. Lucy joins the Callaghans for Christmas and brings what item as a gift?

   A. Fruitcake

   B. Poinsettia

   C. Scented candle

   D. Bottle of wine

7. Walking home from Celeste's New Year's Eve party, Jack eloquently explains the art of what romantic technique?

   A. Leaning

   B. Hugging

   C. Kissing

   D. Flirting

8. What extremely personal detail does Lucy indirectly find out about Peter that convinces his family she knows him intimately?

   A. He has a third nipple

   B. He was adopted

   C. He has only one testicle

   D. He has a birthmark in a specific location

Festive Fact

In Poland, *While You Were Sleeping* is titled *Ja cię kocham, a ty śpisz*, which translates to "I love you and you sleep."

ANSWERS: 1.C, 2.A, 3.D, 4.B, 5.C, 6.B, 7.A, 8.C

SPOTLIGHT QUIZ

Happiest Season

Year: 2020

Director: Clea DuVall

Writers: Clea Duvall, Mary Holland

Cast: Kristen Stewart, Mackenzie Davis, Mary Steenburgen, Victor Garber, Alison Brie

Cheer-O-Meter

Christmas Spirit

Warm Fuzzies

Timelessness

Happiest Season, the semiautobiographical second feature from director Clea DuVall (a queer icon of the nineties for her role in *But I'm a Cheerleader*), was poised to become the first LGBTQIA+ holiday film from a major Hollywood studio . . . that is, until the pandemic hit in 2020. Hulu released the film over Thanksgiving weekend, bringing in more new subscribers to the platform than any other film and becoming Hulu's most-watched original movie during its opening weekend. *Happiest Season* is a breath of fresh air and an important step toward proving there's more than enough room in the Christmas catalog for queer voices, stories, and overall better representation.

1. Abby and Harper go on a walking tour of the 200 Block of Summer Street in Duboistown, Pennsylvania, which goes by what more festive name? The name is shared by the Sia song playing over the action.

    A. Gum Drop Lane

    B. Santa Claus Lane

    C. Candy Cane Lane

    D. Jingle Bell Lane

2. *Schitt's Creek* star and cocreator Daniel Levy steps into the all-important romantic-comedy role of "best friend" to Abby, playing John. Which one of the following facts about John is NOT true?

    A. He's a literary agent

    B. He tracks all his dates and friends (because if the NSA can, so can he)

    C. He's not that great with fish

    D. He hates champagne and other bubbly liquids

3. Abby spends some liquid-therapy time with Riley (played by Aubrey Plaza), Harper's first girlfriend, with an on-point blazer game. They bond together at the Oxwood Bar over the sweet sounds of what festive song?

    A. "Here Comes Santa Claus"

    B. "Must Be Santa"

    C. "Santa Is His Name-O"

    D. "Father Christmas"

4. During the white-elephant exchange at the Caldwells' annual Christmas Eve party, Sloane and Harper burst into the living room and get in a physical fight trying to prevent each other's secrets from being revealed to the family. It comes to a literal breaking point when Harper breaks what handmade gift from Jane over Sloane's head?

    A. A snowflake vase

    B. A gingerbread house

    C. A painting of Main Street

    D. A blown glass ornament

5. The epilogue shows us one year later in the lives of Abby, Harper, and the Caldwell family, where all but which of the following events have taken place?

    A. Ted becomes mayor

    B. Abby and Harper are engaged

    C. The family sees *It's a Wonderful Life* together at the movie theater

    D. Jane is a bestselling author with *Shadow Dreamers and the Second Sister*

The Gift That Keeps on Giving

Giving a gift is a symbolic gesture of our love. Whether you give someone a present that is big or small, it's really the thought that counts. Match these memorable gifts with the movie in which they appear.

1. *A Christmas Prince* (2017)

2. *Serendipity* (2001)

3. *The Best Man Holiday* (2013)

4. *Last Christmas* (2019)

5. *This Is Christmas* (2022)

A. Framed Liverpool Football Club medals

B. A lip-synched performance of "Can You Stand the Rain" by New Edition

C. Black cashmere gloves from Bloomingdale's

D. A pair of sculpted baby Jesuses for Patti LuPone

E. Hand-carved acorn Christmas ornament

ANSWERS: 1.E, 2.C, 3.B, 4.D, 5.A

POST-CREDITS

★ In *Love Actually*, Olivia Olson's rendition of "All I Want for Christmas Is You" (yes, that's her singing) was initially deemed too perfect. Producers had Olson record a simplified version so viewers wouldn't question whether she was really singing.

★ The paperboy shown wiping out on the sidewalk in *While You Were Sleeping* actually fell for real, by accident, and broke his wrist in the process. Director Jon Turteltaub left the outtake in the final cut.

★ Dustin Hoffman's cameo in *The Holiday* was unplanned. The actor was having lunch next door and saw that a movie was shooting. Writer and director Nancy Meyers wrote him into the Blockbuster scene when she realized Miles and Iris were talking about *The Graduate*.

Stocking Stuffer

Christmas TV Specials

Without Christmas TV specials, we wouldn't have Christmas classics like "You're a Mean One, Mr. Grinch" or the piano interlude from A *Charlie Brown Christmas*, and we'd never see what Christmas is like for Garfield, Pee-wee Herman, or Chewbacca's extended family. And we'd surely never be invited into the clearly fake living rooms of Frank Sinatra or Judy Garland to join them at the piano—and neither would David Bowie have been invited to a tense old school versus new school "Little Drummer Boy" sing-off with Bing Crosby.

This quiz highlights a handful of beloved (and one decidedly not beloved) specials that might last less than an hour but leave imprints on our hearts and minds for a lifetime.

A Garfield Christmas (1987)

After gifting Grandma lost love letters from her late husband, Garfield is surprised and overjoyed to receive what Christmas gift from Odie, who secretly built it in the barn?

A Very Murray Christmas (2015)

This homage to classic variety shows was cowritten by former Bill Murray collaborator Mitch Glazer (*Scrooged*) and featured writing/directing from which Oscar-winning filmmaker and Hollywood legacy who once collaborated with Murray in Japan?

Emmet Otter's Jug-Band Christmas (1977)

Emmet's dreams are dashed when his jug band loses the talent show to a last-minute entry featuring members of the Riverbottom Gang known by what band name?

The Guardians of the Galaxy Holiday Special (2022)

For Peter's Christmas present, Drax and Mantis kidnap what Hollywood actor who once saved a small town by dancing like an idiot, received an arrow in the neck from Jason Voorhees, and is the namesake of a popular party game?

Happy Holidays with Bing and Frank (1957)

Before they sing "Jingle Bells," Frank and Bing take a swig of what holiday drink, whose name is derived from a Norse salutation (meaning "be healthy") and is made of ale, apples, and spices and served in a large bowl of the same name?

Olive, the Other Reindeer (1999)

Olive mishears a radio message from Santa Claus and travels to the North Pole to help save Christmas. Olive is an anthropomorphic dog of what popular breed familiar to fans of *Wishbone* and *Frasier*?

Pee-wee's Playhouse Christmas Special (1988)

In this star-studded affair featuring the likes of Cher, Oprah, Little Richard, and Frankie Avalon, Pee-wee goes a little nutty as he repeatedly receives what Christmas gift from his friends?

Star Wars Holiday Special (1978)

This much-maligned cult classic holiday special follows the exploits of Han Solo and Chewbacca as they visit Chewie's home planet of Kashyyyk to celebrate what "day of peace" honoring the values and tenets of Wookiee culture?

The Happy Elf (2005)

Based on the song of the same name by Harry Connick Jr., this film follows Eubie, the titular elf, who tries to get what town with a music-inspired name off the Naughty List?

The Snowman (1982)

When this Oscar nominee and seasonal favorite in England released in America, producers replaced an introduction from author Raymond Briggs with one from which chameleonic pop star, who sprinkled his magic stardust on the film?

ANSWERS: 1. Back scratcher, 2. Sofia Coppola, 3. The Nightmare, 4. Kevin Bacon, 5. Wassail, 6. Jack Russell terrier, 7. Fruitcake, 8. Life Day, 9. Bluesville, 10. David Bowie

Laughing All the Way

COMEDY

Without comedy at Christmastime, we never would have learned the schoolyard wisdom that Batman smells or Robin laid an egg. Without comedy at Christmastime, we wouldn't have the indelible image of Cousin Eddie happily flippering his way into a dream sequence to the tune of "Mele Kalikimaka (Merry Christmas)" while wearing a spotted Speedo. And without comedy at Christmastime, we wouldn't have learned that the only defense against bullies is lying in the snow like a slug.

The best Christmas comedies poke fun at our own tendencies to lose the thread of the Christmas spirit in our preparations. *National Lampoon's Christmas Vacation* has been a Christmas comedy staple for thirty-five years because it taught us that Clark Griswold's greatest gift to the world wasn't a new pool for his family; it was the gift of allowing the audiences to know for just a minute how much worse it really could be. These comedies remind us that amidst the chaos and commercialism, a good laugh and a light heart are what truly keep the spirit of Christmas alive.

A Christmas Story

Year: 1983

Director: Bob Clark

Writers: Jean Shepherd, Leigh Brown, Bob Clark

Cast: Melinda Dillon, Darren McGavin, Peter Billingsley, Ian Petrella, Jean Shepherd

Plot: Set in the 1940s, this Christmas staple follows Ralphie Parker, who has only one wish for Christmas: a Red Ryder BB gun. As he desperately tries to convince his parents that this is the perfect gift, Ralphie experiences the challenges of childhood.

Cheer-O-Meter

Christmas Spirit

Warm Fuzzies

Timelessness

Festive Fact

The iconic tongue-stuck-to-the-flagpole scene was achieved by placing a small piece of plastic with a hole over the flagpole, attached to which was a little vacuum-like motor that became a suction to hold the tongue in place.

1. **Ralphie gets his first glimpse of his most-coveted Christmas gift as he and a crowd of shoppers watch in wonderment at the golden, tinkling display of mechanized, electronic joy in the corner window of what department store?**

   A. Goldblatt's

   B. Dillard's

   C. Higbee's

   D. Herpolsheimer's

2. **Inspired by his father, who once saw a man lick a railroad track, Schwartz goes for the throat by daring Flick to lick a metal flagpole, using what coup de grâce of all dares? The exact exchange and nuance are very important.**

   A.   Quadruple Dog Dare

   B.   Triple Dog Dare

   C.   Double Dare

   D.   Dead Man's Dare

3. **Helping his old man with a blowout tire, Ralphie says "the queen mother of dirty words" and gets a fate worse than the guillotine, the chair, or the rack with what brand of soap shoved in his mouth?**

   A.   Palmolive

   B.   Lux

   C.   Woodbury

   D.   Lifebuoy

4. **Proudly displayed in the front-room window is a lascivious leg lamp in fishnet stockings. This major award sent to the house on Cleveland Street is adorned with what "Italian" phrase on the crate?**

   A.   Delicata

   B.   Fragile

   C.   Rompibile

   D.   Cassable

5. At 6:45 p.m., the one thing that could drag Ralphie from "the soft glow of electric sex gleaming in the window" was what favorite radio program that sent him a secret decoder ring?

A. *The Lone Ranger*

B. *The Black Pirate Ship*

C. *The Adventures of Sherlock Holmes*

D. *Little Orphan Annie*

6. In Hohman, Indiana, you're either a bully, a toady, or one of the nameless rabble of victims. Scut Farkus is a bully, but he doesn't make kids say uncle alone. Who is his partner in crime?

A. Grover Dill

B. Oscar Kirchman

C. Gunner Voda

D. Gordy Dalton

7. Ralphie finally gets an official Red Ryder carbine-action 0range-model air rifle with a compass in the stock and this thing that tells time . . . with how many shots?

A. 320

B. 650

C. 100

D. 200

8. On Christmas morning, Ralphie takes one shot from his Red Ryder and nearly shoots out his eye but is saved by his glasses. What excuse does he give his mother?

A. An icicle fell on him

B. Scut Farkus got his revenge

C. Randy smacked him with his zeppelin

D. A snowball sandwich from Schwartz

Christmas with the Kranks

Year: 2004

Director: Joe Roth

Writer: Chris Columbus

Cast: Tim Allen, Jamie Lee Curtis, Dan Aykroyd, M. Emmet Walsh, Erik Per Sullivan

Plot: Luther and Nora Krank decide to skip Christmas and go on a cruise, causing an uproar among their Christmas-obsessed neighbors. When they receive word that their daughter will be back home for Christmas, Luther and Nora rush to make sure it's perfect.

Cheer-O-Meter

Christmas Spirit

Warm Fuzzies

Timelessness

1. Luther and Nora Krank have trouble acclimating to life as empty nesters due to their daughter, Blair, joining the Peace Corps and flying to what country the day after Thanksgiving?

    A. Panama

    B. Peru

    C. Paraguay

    D. Philippines

2. After doing some calculations, Luther realizes too much money is spent every holiday season and proposes that he and Nora skip Christmas. How much money did they spend the previous Christmas?

   A. $4,132

   B. $5,132

   C. $6,132

   D. $7,132

3. Vic Frohmeyer, the unelected boss of the street, hears that the Kranks stiffed the Boy Scouts selling Christmas trees and forms an alliance to force the Kranks to put up what kind of decoration matching the neighborhood?

   A. Frosty the Snowman

   B. Rudolph the Red-Nosed Reindeer

   C. Santa Claus

   D. The Grinch

4. St. Maria's Lutheran Church has a truck full of carolers who arrive in the neighborhood and are strongly encouraged by Walt to sing on Luther and Nora's lawn. What Christmas carol do they sing to Luther's annoyance?

   A. "Deck the Halls"

   B. "Joy to the World"

   C. "Jingle Bells"

   D. "Carol of the Bells"

5. Where does Nora volunteer and read *How the Grinch Stole Christmas!* when Luther shows up, unable to move his face from Botox injections?

   A. A children's library

   B. A children's shelter

   C. A children's play place

   D. A children's hospital

Festive Fact

The film takes place in the historic town of Riverside, Illinois, but to have less unpredictable weather, it was filmed on a fake exterior street built on a parking lot of a former Boeing aircraft factory in Downey, California.

6. While frantically shopping, Nora gets into a battle with a shopper, bribes a young mother, and almost gets hit by a truck that destroys what special food item, forcing her to buy smoked trout?

    A.   Hickory honey ham

    B.   Cajun-seasoned turkey

    C.   Christmas prime rib

    D.   Rolled shoulder pork

7. Realizing that he wasn't grateful enough for the support of his friends and family, Luther gives his neighbor Walt and Walt's ailing wife, Bev, what no-strings-attached Christmas offering?

    A.   All the money he saved for Christmas

    B.   His cruise tickets to the Caribbean

    C.   A private sleigh ride through town

    D.   A new puppy to be friends with their cat Muffles

8. Marty, the kind shopper at the store whom Nora invites to the party, is shown at the beginning of the film selling what item?

    A.   Umbrellas

    B.   Holiday calendars

    C.   Christmas trees

    D.   Fruitcakes

Just Friends

Cheer-O-Meter

Christmas Spirit

Warm Fuzzies

Timelessness

Year: 2005

Director: Roger Kumble

Writer: Adam "Tex" Davis

Cast: Ryan Reynolds, Amy Smart, Anna Faris, Christopher Marquette, Chris Klein

Plot: Former high school nerd Chris unavoidably returns home for Christmas and is determined to win over his high school crush, Jamie, who had previously put him firmly in the friend zone.

1. The film opens in New Jersey, 1995, when unpopular nerd Chris is writing a heartfelt yearbook message to his longtime friend and crush, Jamie. What song is Chris singing until his brother interrupts him?

   A. "I Swear" by All-4-One

   B. "I'll Make Love to You" by Boyz II Men

   C. "All My Life" by K-Ci & JoJo

   D. "Back at One" by Brian McKnight

Festive Fact

The film was shot in Regina, Saskatchewan, in frigid temperatures that reached lows in the negative thirties and forties Fahrenheit.

2. Ten years after being humiliated by his classmates, Chris is now a successful record executive tasked with signing self-obsessed pop star Samantha James. What causes his plane to catch fire, forcing Chris to return home and face his past?

A. Sashimi and aluminum foil

B. Salmon and aluminum foil

C. Ahi tuna and aluminum foil

D. Risotto and aluminum foil

3. Chris and Jamie go out for lunch to reconnect at a neighborhood restaurant "where they have history." The waitress recognizes Chris, brings him his usual Sugar Mountain Supreme, and calls him what nickname?

A. Tubby Tiger

B. Chubby Bunny

C. Chunky Monkey

D. Pudgy Penguin

4. When Chris tries to impress Jamie during a children's hockey game, a rogue puck smacks him in the teeth and knocks him out. The paramedic who saves the day is former pimple-faced and stammering classmate Dusty, who has what last name?

A. Twinkleman

B. Finkleman

C. Winkleman

D. Dinkleman

5. After acting like one of Jamie's high school boyfriends backfires on him, Chris tries to unlock his former sensitive side. He asks Jamie out on a Christmas Eve date, with Dusty and his mother tagging along, to see what movie?

A. *The Notebook*

B. *Beaches*

C. *A Walk to Remember*

D. *Ghost*

6. Jamie and Chris separately complain to Darla and Clark about their feelings for each other, with Jamie saying she tried what special move on Chris that didn't work?

   A. The cold-ears move

   B. The chapped-lips move

   C. The sore-back move

   D. The cold-feet move

7. In front of a church full of children, Chris provokes Dusty, and they have a physical fight that leads to them falling on top of and breaking what item displayed for the congregation?

   A. Nativity scene

   B. Votive candles

   C. Gingerbread houses

   D. Snow globes

8. Dusty finally shows his true colors, and when Chris gloats about it, he drunkenly offends Jamie and gets slapped, punched, and thrown out of what neighborhood bar where Jamie works part-time?

   A. The Redwood Tavern

   B. The Maple Tavern

   C. The Willow Tavern

   D. The Elm Tavern

Festive Fact

Stars Ryan Reynolds and Amy Smart reunited eighteen years after the film's release for a "Happy Just Friendsgiving" ad for Reynolds's gin company, Aviation American Gin.

ANSWERS: 1.A, 2.C, 3.B, 4.D, 5.A, 6.D, 7.C, 8.B

National Lampoon's Christmas Vacation

Cheer-O-Meter

Christmas Spirit

Warm Fuzzies

Timelessness

Year: 1989

Director: Jeremiah S. Chechik

Writer: John Hughes

Cast: Chevy Chase, Beverly D'Angelo, Randy Quaid, Juliette Lewis, Johnny Galecki

Plot: Clark Griswold's plan for a good old-fashioned family Christmas hilariously unravels into a chaotic but well-intentioned family gathering in Chicago. This classic comes complete with obnoxious in-laws, selfish bosses, and enough Christmas lights to be seen from space.

1. **As the family stands outside, Clark unveils his dedication to the Griswold family Christmas with a light display. After several unsuccessful attempts, how many imported Italian twinkle lights shine from the house?**

   A. 10,000

   B. 15,000

   C. 20,000

   D. 25,000

2. The Griswolds' snooty neighbors get a rogue icicle through their window that destroys their expensive Bang & Olufsen stereo. This is where we first learn their names. Complete the quote: "And why is the carpet all wet, ____?" "I don't know, ____!"

   A. Todd/Margo

   B. Rob/Marla

   C. Beau/Ani

   D. Chad/Cleo

3. During the silent majesty of a winter's morn with the clean, cool chill of the holiday air, Clark notices an idiot (Cousin Eddie) in his bathrobe emptying a chemical toilet into his sewer. How does Eddie greet Clark through the window?

   A. "Crapper was full!"

   B. "Toilet was full!"

   C. "Pisser was full!"

   D. "Sh*tter was full!"

4. The film takes place in the Chicago suburbs, so naturally there are some references to the beloved local sports teams, including which team's jersey that is worn by both Clark and his son, Rusty?

   A. Chicago Bears

   B. Chicago Blackhawks

   C. Chicago Bulls

   D. Chicago Cubs

5. All but which of the following facts about Aunt Bethany are true?

   A. She shared a peanut-butter-and-banana sandwich with Elvis

   B. The Pledge of Allegiance is her preferred dinner blessing

   C. She wrapped up her cat and her Jell-O mold as presents

   D. She's always concerned about breaking wind

6. Expecting a big Christmas bonus check, Clark feels punched in the face by his boss when he learns he received what one-year membership as a gift? As Cousin Eddie says, it's the gift that keeps on giving.

    A. Nuts of the Month Club

    B. Beer of the Month Club

    C. Jelly of the Month Club

    D. Steak of the Month Club

7. Clark has a full-blown four-alarm emergency holiday breakdown and goes on an epic rant about his bloodsucking, snake-licking, spotty-lipped, worm-headed sack of a boss. This iconic monologue ends with him asking for what medicine?

    A. Motrin

    B. Aspirin

    C. Tums

    D. Tylenol

8. The party ends with not one but two bangs (sort of) with the Griswold family Christmas tree burning to a crisp and Clark's Santa and reindeer decoration blowing up and flying in the sky. What partygoer was responsible?

    A. The lost squirrel

    B. Aunt Bethany's cat

    C. Uncle Lewis

    D. Cousin Eddie

Festive Fact

According to Beverly D'Angelo (who plays Ellen), when Clark is going on his rant, the cast behind the camera had cue cards hanging around their necks by a rope just in case Chevy needed the lines. Watch Chevy's eyes naturally moving, and you'll see them go from person to person during one stretch.

Surviving Christmas

Cheer-O-Meter

Christmas Spirit

Warm Fuzzies

Timelessness

Year: 2004

Director: Mike Mitchell

Writers: Deborah Kaplan, Harry Elfont, Jennifer Ventimilia, Joshua Sternin

Cast: Ben Affleck, James Gandolfini, Christina Applegate, Catherine O'Hara, Josh Zuckerman

Plot: Humorously exploring the lengths to which one will go to avoid loneliness during the festive season, this film follows Drew, a wealthy executive who pays a family living in his childhood home to pretend they're his own for Christmas.

1. The film opens with wealthy advertising executive Drew pitching a new commercial for what holiday product?

   A. Peterman's Peppermint Mocha

   B. Noggerton's Eggnog

   C. Connie's Cocoa Bliss

   D. Fosch's Fruitcake

2. What pre-Christmas gift from Drew to his girlfriend, Missy, effectively ends their relationship?

   A. First-class tickets to Fiji

   B. First-class tickets to the Caribbean

   C. First-class tickets to Brazil

   D. First-class tickets to Mexico

3. Hoping not to spend Christmas alone, Drew takes a taxi to his hometown of Lincolnwood, Illinois, and offers the Valco family how much money to pretend he's their son for Christmas?

A. $100,000

B. $50,000

C. $250,000

D. $150,000

4. Drew tries to help by arranging a very hip and very sexy yet tasteful photo shoot to show Christine that she's beautiful. What rock song plays in the background during the session?

A. "Pour Some Sugar on Me" by Def Leppard

B. "Back in Black" by AC/DC

C. "Cherry Pie" by Warrant

D. "Sweet Child of Mine" by Guns N' Roses

5. The first time that Drew and Alicia bond is when they do what winter activity together that gets them both sick?

A. Ice skating

B. Snowboarding

C. Polar plunge

D. Sledding

6. What did Christine see in the park as a child, a memory that she still carries with her?

A. A live Nativity scene

B. A tree with icicle branches

C. A group of reindeer sliding down a hill

D. The perfect Christmas tree

7. When Missy leaves after a disastrous surprise visit, what memento from Drew does she say she's keeping?

A. The Cartier bracelet

B. The Tiffany ring

C. The Bentley

D. The Harry Winston necklace

8. Which of the following revelations did Drew NOT tell Christine when she pressed him on why he would rather spend Christmas with a fake family than his real family?

A. His dad walked out on him at Christmas when he was four

B. He never actually had a Doo-Dah

C. He hasn't spoken to his brother in twenty-five years

D. His late mom always worked Christmas at a twenty-four-hour diner

SPOTLIGHT QUIZ

The Holdovers

Year: 2023

Director: Alexander Payne

Writer: David Hemingson

Cast: Paul Giamatti, Da'Vine Joy Randolph, Dominic Sessa, Carrie Preston, Gillian Vigman

Released in 2023, *The Holdovers*—Oscar winner Alexander Payne's second collaboration with actor Paul Giamatti (*Sideways*)—not only became an awards darling but also had all the trimmings to become a new holiday classic thanks to the performances of its three leads, the exceptional script, and the 1970s aesthetics, which felt like the warm embrace of nostalgia. Loosely based on Marcel Pagnol's 1935 French film *Merlusse*, Payne's story pairs mistletoe with a memorable misanthrope who befriends a troubled student and troubled coworker stuck at a boarding school over the holidays in frigid Massachusetts. Blending the right amount of cynicism and sentimentality, the film expertly touches on grief, class, race, entitlement, selflessness, and most of all, loneliness.

Cheer-O-Meter

Christmas Spirit

Warm Fuzzies

Timelessness

1. **Mary has been grieving the loss of her son (a Barton alum), who died in the Vietnam War. Like Hunham, she remains closed off to the outside world, until one night, when they find themselves bonding over what television show?**

   A. *The Dating Game*

   B. *Family Feud*

   C. *The Newlywed Game*

   D. *Match Game*

2. When Hunham catches Angus trying to arrange a hotel room, he chases him around the school but struggles to keep up. At one point, Angus enters the off-limits gymnasium and jumps on a gymnastic springboard, landing on the floor and sustaining what injury?

    A. Breaks his wrist

    B. Twists his ankle

    C. Breaks his collarbone

    D. Dislocates his shoulder

3. Hunham does his best to make Christmas special for Mary and Angus by picking up a tiny tree and gifting them what book that, for his money, is like "the Bible, the Koran, and the Bhagavad Gita all rolled up into one"?

    A. *Meditations* by Marcus Aurelius

    B. *Meditations* by Julius Caesar

    C. *Meditations* by Demosthenes

    D. *Meditations* by Cicero

4. After a visit to a bar where Hunham deescalates a situation with some Vietnam soldiers, Angus tells him that he stinks. Hunham reveals to Angus that he's always struggled with trimethylaminuria, a rare genetic condition that generates what unpleasant smell?

    A. Cheese

    B. Fish

    C. Asparagus

    D. Onions

5. Angus requests a field trip to Boston, and Hunham reluctantly agrees. Before returning back to Barton, Angus visits his father, who lives in a sanatorium. What gift does Angus give his father that ultimately is the reason he and Hunham get in trouble?

    A. A Zippo lighter

    B. A hippo paperweight

    C. A snow globe

    D. An antique pen

JINGLE BELL BONUS
Extended Holiday Hours

Working during the holidays comes with its own brand of ridiculousness, from angry customers to worrying you won't make it home in time for presents. Comedies show us just how funny it can be. Can you match the film title with the type of business that's featured in the film?

1. *Deck the Halls* (2006)
2. *Comfort and Joy* (1984)
3. *Mixed Nuts* (1994)
4. *All Is Bright* (2013)
5. *Friday after Next* (2002)

A. A Christmas tree shop
B. A suicide prevention hotline
C. A BBQ restaurant
D. A car dealership
E. An ice cream van

POST-CREDITS

★ In **National Lampoon's Christmas Vacation**, Chevy Chase broke his pinky finger while punching the blow-mold Santa and reindeer on the front lawn when the lights weren't working. After he sustained the injury, he continued kicking because it hurt so much and he didn't want to ruin the take.

★ **Christmas with the Kranks** is based on the novel *Skipping Christmas* by bestselling novelist John Grisham. The film's title was changed so it wouldn't be confused with the Ben Affleck Christmas movie *Surviving Christmas*.

★ **The Holdovers** is the first film for actor Dominic Sessa (who plays Angus). Casting director Susan Shopmaker gave students at his school, Deerfield Academy (one of the locations standing in for Barton Academy), a chance to audition for a role. Sessa impressed everyone on the film and got his big break.

Home for The Holidays

FAMILY DYSFUNCTION

There's no place like home for the holidays. At least that's what Perry Como says. There's nothing better than chewing on some homemade brownies with your mom while watching Hollywood stars chew on the scenery of an epic dinner table scene where stunning revelations come to light. At home, you get your eccentric uncle talking about Bitcoin. In the movies, Sarah Jessica Parker puts her foot in her mouth in an epically cringe moment. Everyone's family has their own issues—that's what makes a family special. And if fictional families can handle the most stressful situations, then perhaps you can too.

Maybe Brad and Kate from *Four Christmases* had the right idea in attempting to escape their families and fly five thousand miles away. But if they had succeeded, there wouldn't be a movie, and we wouldn't be curled up on the couch spending time with our families and laughing about all the crazy situations the characters get themselves into. These films showcase the joy, chaos, and heartwarming moments that unfold when we, and our favorite movie characters, heed Perry Como's timeless advice and journey back to our roots, reaffirming that home is indeed where the heart—and the heart of the holidays—truly lies.

Daddy's Home 2

Year: 2017

Director: Sean Anders

Writers: Sean Anders, John Morris

Cast: Will Ferrell, Mark Wahlberg, Linda Cardellini, John Lithgow, Mel Gibson

Plot: In this holiday sequel to *Daddy's Home,* co-dads Dusty and Brad join forces to try to provide the perfect Christmas for their kids. But their newfound partnership is put to the test when their own fathers arrive.

1. With the annual Christmas pageant approaching, Dusty and Brad seem to have coparenting down. Brad reminds Dusty to make a homemade treat for the event and brings him what festive drink to warm his spirits during after-school pickup?

    A. Peppermint mocha

    B. Hot apple cider

    C. Hot cocoa

    D. Eggnog latte

Cheer-O-Meter

Christmas Spirit

Warm Fuzzies

Timelessness

Festive Fact

The film's cinematographer was Julio Macat, whose big break was shooting *Home Alone*. Perhaps his most personally memorable film was the remake of *Miracle on 34th Street*, where he met his wife, actress Elizabeth Perkins.

2. Dusty's father, Kurt, makes a surprise appearance for the holidays. Envious that his grandchildren call Brad's dad "Pop-Pop," Kurt requests that moving forward he's referred to as what?

    A. El Guapo

    B. El Padre

    C. El Capitán

    D. El Lobo

3. What sacred covenant does Adrianna break at the family Airbnb that surprisingly has Kurt, Don, and Brad all in agreement?

    A. Wasting water

    B. Leaving lights on

    C. Not closing doors

    D. Touching the thermostat

4. Brad nearly dies trying to cut down a Christmas tree on public lands and ends up having to pay $20,000 for it because it contained what nontraditional Christmas accoutrement?

    A. A 4G cell-phone tower

    B. A family of endangered eagles

    C. A carving by George Washington

    D. Toxic waste

5. Thanks to Kurt's influence, what present does Dylan initially ask the neighborhood Santa for? The present ends up putting Kurt in the hospital, but he's even prouder than before.

    A. Bow and arrow

    B. Bowie knife

    C. Twenty-gauge shotgun

    D. Samurai sword

6. To diffuse tensions, Brad suggests the men have a Dads' Night Out and do what activity to bond? It's here that Brad learns his parents are divorcing.

  A. Gingerbread-house contest

  B. Christmas burlesque

  C. Santa bar crawl

  D. Improv show

7. When a blizzard prevents everyone from leaving town, a Christmas-themed action film titled *Missile Tow* brings the family together, helping them share their true feelings for each other. What Hollywood actor provides his voice for this fictional film?

  A. Jason Statham

  B. Keanu Reeves

  C. Liam Neeson

  D. Jean-Claude Van Damme

8. In the movie theater lobby, Brad inspires everyone to come together and have the greatest Christmas party ever. What song (which was featured earlier as one that haunted Dusty in Glee Club) is revealed to be Roger's favorite song?

  A. "Do They Know It's Christmas?" by Band Aid

  B. "Last Christmas" by Wham!

  C. "White Christmas" by Bing Crosby

  D. "Wonderful Christmastime" by Paul McCartney

Festive Fact

There's a post-credits scene featuring John Lithgow's character, Don, doing what he does best: talking too much. He bores a group of Nativity actors, who leave him alone in the manger.

Four Christmases

Year: 2008

Director: Seth Gordon

Writers: Matt R. Allen, Caleb Wilson, Jon Lucas, Scott Moore

Cast: Vince Vaughn, Reese Witherspoon, Robert Duvall, Jon Favreau, Mary Steenburgen

Plot: Brad and Kate's plan to escape their family for a tropical Christmas getaway falls apart and leads to an unexpected marathon of four separate family celebrations.

Cheer-O-Meter

Christmas Spirit

Warm Fuzzies

Timelessness

1. Unmarried couple Brad and Kate are trying to avoid family for the holidays, so they pretend they are inoculating babies in Burma so they can take a flight to what idyllic location?

   A. Bora Bora

   B. Aruba

   C. Fiji

   D. Bermuda

Festive Fact

Peter Billingsley, best known for playing Ralphie in *A Christmas Story*, makes a cameo as the ticket agent who prevents Brad and Kate from traveling on the holiday. He also served as an executive producer.

2. **Brad and Katie's first stop is with Brad's father and his semiprofessional cage-fighting Neanderthal brothers. What safe word does Brad give to Kate in case his family is too much for her?**

   A. Mistletoe

   B. Eggnog

   C. Frosty

   D. Blitzen

3. **What special Christmas present does Brad get his father (without knowing the ten-dollar limit) that results in a completely trashed living room and a fire in the house?**

   A. Satellite dish

   B. 60-inch plasma TV

   C. Rotisserie-chicken oven

   D. Reclining chair with keg

4. **While Kate was a kid, she was trapped inside a bounce house and tormented by a bunch of kids. She has PTSD when she sees a bounce house at her mother's. What does Kate call this torture device?**

   A. Bounce-bounce

   B. Boing-boing

   C. Hop-hop

   D. Jump-jump

5. **Marilyn, Kate's mother, has a new beau: Pastor Phil. One of his biggest influences (aside from a Jesus on the front lawn) is what new rule about Christmas?**

   A. Abstinence for all of December

   B. All carols have to be sung in original Latin

   C. No presents, just verbal gift giving

   D. All food must be vegan

6. At Pastor Phil's megachurch, Brad gives an inspired performance onstage, playing what role given to him at the last minute? Kate is also given a role but has major stage fright, just like she did when playing a tree in *Pippin*.

   A. Jesus

   B. Joseph

   C. King Herod

   D. The Angel Gabriel

7. Kate meets Brad's mother, Paula, and Paula's much younger boyfriend, Darryl, who is also Brad's former best friend. They all play what game, which reveals more truths than anyone was prepared for?

   A. Taboo

   B. Scattergories

   C. Pictionary

   D. Fibbage

8. After realizing they want to have kids after all, Brad and Kate have a baby on what holiday, causing them once again to be on live TV and to risk their families finding out?

   A. Valentine's Day

   B. The Fourth of July

   C. Christmas

   D. New Year's Day

Festive Fact

All four parents in the film are Oscar winners: Sissy Spacek, Robert Duvall, Mary Steenburgen, and Jon Voight. Three actors in the film won Oscars for playing country singers: Reese Witherspoon, Robert Duvall, and Sissy Spacek. Two actors in the film are country singers: Dwight Yoakam and Tim McGraw. And one is a Tony Award–winning Broadway star: Kristin Chenoweth.

ANSWERS: 1.C, 2.A, 3.A, 4.D, 5.C, 6.B, 7.A, 8.D

Nothing Like the Holidays

Year: 2008

Director: Alfredo De Villa

Writers: Rick Najera, Ted Perkins, Alison Swan

Cast: John Leguizamo, Debra Messing, Freddy Rodriguez, Alfred Molina, Elizabeth Peña

Plot: Members of a tight-knit Puerto Rican family in Chicago gather for the holidays where a stunning revelation is uncovered and the family grapples with the possibility that this Christmas could be their last together.

Cheer-O-Meter

Christmas Spirit

Warm Fuzzies

Timelessness

1. Jesse Rodriguez, a marine returning home from Iraq, is picked up from the airport and requests to make what stop upon returning to the Humboldt Park neighborhood of Chicago?

   A. A food truck to get plátanos

   B. A park to play baseball

   C. A store to buy a present for his father

   D. A shelter to give out food

Festive Fact

If you'd like to visit the Rodriguez home and see if the tree still stands, it's located at 2329 North Monticello Avenue in Chicago.

2. During their first holiday dinner back together as a family, Anna, the matriarch of the family, drops what bombshell, causing an immediate rift between everyone at the table?

   A. "We're selling the house."

   B. "I have lung cancer."

   C. "I'm divorcing your father."

   D. "Mauricio was adopted."

3. Edy convinces the men to help him cut down the giant tree and eyesore in the front yard, which Anna has hated for twenty-five years. Fernando brings a large chainsaw that he proudly boasts has what action star on its box?

   A. Arnold Schwarzenegger

   B. Sylvester Stallone

   C. Clint Eastwood

   D. Chuck Norris

4. When the family gets a surprise visit from Father Torres, Sarah takes care of dinner and gets what kind of takeout due to her inability to cook? This is a thorn in Anna's side when it comes to her Jewish daughter-in-law.

   A. Chinese

   B. Burgers and fries

   C. Pizza

   D. Pancakes

5. What family business does Edy own that he expects Jesse to take over once he returns from Iraq? He even changes the name of it to *Edy and Son* to entice him.

   A. Diner

   B. Auto repair shop

   C. Bodega

   D. Dry cleaners

6. The family excitedly joins together for a Christmas parade on their way to a huge party. What song, along with "The First Noel," does the parade sing in joyous harmony?

    A. "O Come, All Ye Faithful"

    B. "Mil Felicidades"

    C. "We Wish You a Merry Christmas"

    D. "O Little Town of Bethlehem"

7. At the Christmas party, Edy sees Anna dancing with another man and gets a bit jealous, but not as jealous as what character who starts a fight with Jesse over his lover?

    A. Johnny

    B. Mauricio

    C. Ozzy

    D. Fernando

8. After delivering some Christmas presents to Marissa, Jesse sits on a bench and calls the parents of what friend and fellow soldier, whose death in Iraq he feels guilty about?

    A. Wade

    B. Kirch

    C. Lenny

    D. Jimmy

Festive Fact

The parade shown in the film is called a *parranda*, a Puerto Rican Christmas caroling tradition where friends and family sing *aguinaldos* (or Christmas songs) and enjoy coquitos, a Puerto Rican eggnog beverage. The party goes from house to house and continually grows.

The Family Stone

Cheer-O-Meter

Christmas Spirit

Warm Fuzzies

Timelessness

Year: 2005

Director: Thomas Bezucha

Writer: Thomas Bezucha

Cast: Claire Danes, Diane Keaton, Rachel McAdams, Dermot Mulroney, Sarah Jessica Parker

Plot: When the eldest Stone son brings his conservative girlfriend home for Christmas, her presence sends ripples through the holiday.

1. Meredith runs off to her room feeling embarrassed during what game the family plays together?

   A. Scrabble

   B. Monopoly

   C. Pictionary

   D. Charades

2. Before Meredith checks into the inn, carefree Ben approaches her in Everett's car and tells her that he had a dream about her. He also gives her what item of Sybil's that Sybil will kill her for if she doesn't return?

   A. Her scarf

   B. Her coat

   C. Her mug

   D. Her laptop

3. Julie, Meredith's sister, arrives in town to join the family for Christmas and makes what grand entrance, setting Everett's heart aflutter?

   A. She falls into his arms

   B. She mistakenly hits on him

   C. She falls off a bus

   D. She twirls her hair

4. What wisdom does Ben give Meredith after she crashes Everett's car?

   A. Let your freak flag fly

   B. Own your mistakes

   C. Treat failures as lessons

   D. Warm beer is still good beer

5. Which of the following Christmas gifts was NOT received by one of the Stone family members on Christmas Day?

   A. A clock radio

   B. A houndstooth blazer

   C. A framed photo of Sybil pregnant with Amy

   D. A snow globe

6. Sybil gives Everett what Christmas present he wanted at the beginning of the film?

   A. Her mother's wedding dress

   B. Her mother's journal

   C. Her mother's wedding ring

   D. Her mother's watch

7. What dish is the reason for Sybil, Meredith, Amy, Ben, and Everett all ending up on the kitchen floor?

   A. Quiche

   B. Strata

   C. Lasagna

   D. Moussaka

8. It's one year later and Thad and his partner, Patrick, introduce their new son to Kelly, who calls him King what?

   A. Gus

   B. Jackson

   C. Sully

   D. Max

ANSWERS: 1.D, 2.C, 3.C, 4.A, 5.A, 6.C, 7.B, 8.A

This Christmas

Year: 2007

Director: Preston A. Whitmore II

Writer: Preston A. Whitmore II

Cast: Delroy Lindo, Idris Elba, Loretta Devine, Regina King, Columbus Short

Plot: The Whitfields are back together for Christmas for the first time in years. As each sibling returns home, they must confront their past and rekindle the festive joy and unity that has been strained since their patriarch abandoned them.

Cheer-O-Meter

Christmas Spirit

Warm Fuzzies

Timelessness

1. Lisa and Kelli get into an argument when Lisa proposes that it would be a big help if they sell the family business that Ma'Dere has been running for twenty years. What kind of business does every member of the family have a percentage in?

   A. Restaurant

   B. Dry cleaning

   C. Car wash

   D. Antique store

Festive Fact

Actress Sharon Leal starred in the film adaptation of the Broadway musical *Dreamgirls* a year earlier, which featured a cameo from her *This Christmas* castmate Loretta Devine, who played the role of Lorrell Robinson in the original Broadway production of *Dreamgirls*.

2. After a tension-filled conversation with Joe in the garage, Quentin, Ma'Dere's eldest son and a traveling musician, opens up the piano to play a rendition of what holiday classic to the delight of his mother?

   A. "Silent Night"

   B. "Christmas Time Is Here"

   C. "Winter Wonderland"

   D. "The Christmas Song"

3. Which of the Whitfield women gets a little jollier than anticipated one night and "technically" sleeps with Santa and gives him her cookies?

   A. Kelli

   B. Mel

   C. Lisa

   D. Ma'Dere

4. Sandi, Claude's secret wife and Ma'Dere's surprise daughter-in-law, arrives at the house and is immediately comforted by Mel, who finds out that Sandi is dealing with all but which of the following issues?

   A. Claude is AWOL

   B. Her own family doesn't like Claude because he's a Marine

   C. Claude is in jail

   D. She's a newlywed and pregnant

5. Quentin tries to sneak out of town by train but gets jumped by Mo and Dude, bookies to whom he owes $25,000. Joe steps in and saves the day, giving them how much cash to end it all?

   A. $5,000

   B. $7,000

   C. $10,000

   D. $25,000

6. When Malcolm comes home from his tryst in New York, Lisa confronts him about his infidelity by telling him she drove his prized Escalade into the LA River and beats him with a belt until he leaves town. But what secret ingredient does Lisa get from Ma'Dere that pulls it all together?

   A. Photographs

   B. Rope

   C. Phone records

   D. Baby oil

Festive Fact

During the final Soul Train line, Chris Brown dances with a framed photo. It's the high school graduation photo of actress Lauren London.

7. Baby receives the first gift of the film and provides the last gift of the film by performing the titular song as a surprise to Ma'Dere. But what gift does Baby wrap for the entire family earlier?

   A. A Christmas photo album

   B. A demo of his first album

   C. A hand-drawn portrait of Senior, his father

   D. A sentimental letter about wanting to be a singer

8. The entire cast reunites before the end credits in front of a Christmas tree for a Soul Train line to what song that, thanks to this movie, should be added to the Christmas playlist?

   A. "Dance to the Music" by Sly & the Family Stone

   B. "Got to Give It Up" by Marvin Gaye

   C. "Now That We Found Love" by Heavy D & The Boyz

   D. "Give Me the Night" by George Benson

SPOTLIGHT QUIZ

Single All the Way

Year: 2021

Director: Michael Mayer

Writer: Chad Hodge

Cast: Michael Urie, Philemon Chambers, Luke Macfarlane, Jennifer Coolidge, Kathy Najimy

Plot: The GLAAD Media Award–winning *Single All the Way* is Netflix's first gay holiday rom-com, marking a significant shift toward inclusive storytelling. The film champions a positive queer message that's long overdue in mainstream releases. It eschews the worn narratives of queer trauma, homophobic families, and dramatic struggles with identity for a story about two gay men falling in love in a town that isn't homophobic surrounded by genuinely loving and supportive family. This Netflix gem is a progressive leap, affirming that queer stories deserve a prime spot in the holiday canon, aligning with the true spirit of the season—open hearts and open hearths for all.

Cheer-O-Meter

Christmas Spirit

Warm Fuzzies

Timelessness

1. Nick finds inspiration during his time in New Hampshire with Peter's family to write what sequel to his successful book, *Saving Emmett*?

    A. *Emmett Moves to New Hampshire*

    B. *Emmett at the Christmas Hotel*

    C. *Emmett and the Christmas Pageant*

    D. *Emmett and His Two Dads*

2. Before Aunt Sandy's Christmas Nativity pageant titled *Jesus H. Christ*, she gives a speech to all the actors that Peter realizes is a word-for-word copy of what artist's speech to their backup dancers?

   A. Madonna's preshow prayer from *Madonna: Truth or Dare*

   B. Beyonce's preshow prayer from *Homecoming*

   C. Cher's preshow prayer from *Cher: Live in Concert from Las Vegas*

   D. Taylor's preshow prayer from *Miss Americana*

3. What Christmas song do Peter and his nieces, Sofia and Daniela, have a fully choreographed routine for that they perform in front of Nick and his two nephews?

   A. "All I Want for Christmas Is You" by Mariah Carey

   B. "Merry Christmas, Happy Holidays" by *NSYNC

   C. "My Only Wish (This Year)" by Britney Spears

   D. "Christmas Time" by Christina Aguilera

4. Greeting Peter and Nick at Peter's New Hampshire home is his mother, who insists on being called "Christmas Carol" and is obsessed with what crafting activity?

   A. T-shirt making

   B. Scarf making

   C. Candle making

   D. Sign making

5. When Peter realizes he's in love with Nick, he frantically searches for him. He finds him in an empty storefront, where Nick reveals that he wants to move to New Hampshire with Peter and gives him the keys to what kind of business?

   A. Plant store

   B. Social media firm

   C. Christmas tree lot

   D. Photography studio

ANSWERS: 1.B, 2.A, 3.C, 4.D, 5.A

JINGLE BELL BONUS
Merry Mixtape

It doesn't feel like Christmas until you hear the classic tunes from Bing, Brenda, and Darlene, and it's not a Christmas movie without a really good soundtrack to enhance the story. Can you match these Christmas playlists to the movies in which they appear?

1. *Almost Christmas* (2016)

2. *Boxing Day* (2021)

3. *I'll Be Home for Christmas* (1998)

4. *Love the Coopers* (2015)

5. *Your Christmas or Mine?* (2022) + *Your Christmas or Mine 2* (2023)

A. "Merry Christmas, Happy Holidays" by *NSYNC, "Cool Yule" by Cherry Poppin' Daddies, "Blue Christmas" by Buddy Guy

B. "Rockin' around the Christmas Tree" by Priya Ragu, "Together This Christmas" by Maisie Peters, "You're Christmas to Me" by Sam Ryder

C. "The Light of Christmas Day" by Alison Krauss and Robert Plant, "Carol of the Bells" by Sixpence None the Richer, "If Not for You" by Bob Dylan

D. "Tender Love" by Force MDs, "The Very Thought of You" by Etta James, "Let It Whip" by The Dazz Band

E. "I Say a Little Prayer" by Leigh-Anne Pinnock, "They Gonna Talk" by Beres Hammond, "Never Too Much" by Luther Vandross

POST-CREDITS

⭐ Tyrone Giordano, who plays Thad Stone in **The Family Stone**, is deaf just like his character and helped cast members in sign language classes so the family would be convincing on-screen.

⭐ **Nothing Like the Holidays** was filmed in Chicago's Humboldt Park neighborhood, which is the center of Puerto Rican culture in Chicago. The film even highlights the "Paseo Boricua," a stretch of Division Street where two metal Puerto Rican flags arch over the street at each end.

⭐ Kevin the Snow Plow Guy in **Single All the Way** is played by Dan Finnerty of the cult comedy group The Dan Band, who gained notoriety for a foul-mouthed rendition of "Total Eclipse of the Heart" in *Old School*.

Seeing Is Believing

ANIMATED CHRISTMAS MOVIES

Whether you're four, fourteen, or forty—a grown-up with kids or a kid at heart—anyone can enjoy the magic of an animated Christmas movie during the holidays.

Animated Christmas movies immerse us in worlds where Santa Claus runs a militaristic operation with thousands of elves to deliver presents worldwide; where a bedtime journey to the North Pole gets you back in time for Christmas morning; and where children set aside differences, decorate a tree together, and sing a carol celebrating the true meaning of Christmas. Each movie in this chapter, whether twenty-six minutes or two hours long, brings with it an indisputable aura of Christmas magic that leaves long-lasting memories. There's a reason *A Charlie Brown Christmas* has aired since its 1965 debut and why we all believe in an extraordinary train that stops on our front lawn, giving us a front-row ticket to meet Santa.

Now it's time to snuggle under a blanket with hot cocoa—don't forget the marshmallows!—and let the animated spirit of Christmas whisk you away to an enchanting new world of wonder and whimsy that can melt even the iciest of hearts.

A Charlie Brown Christmas

Cheer-O-Meter

Christmas Spirit

Warm Fuzzies

Timelessness

Year: 1965

Director: Bill Melendez

Writer: Charles M. Schulz

Cast: Peter Robbins, Christopher Shea, Kathy Steinberg, Tracy Stratford, Chris Doran

Plot: In this timeless animated classic, Charlie Brown is on a quest to discover the true meaning of Christmas and, along with the Peanuts gang, navigates the season's joys and challenges.

1. This beloved special opens with Charlie and Linus making their way down to join their friends in what festive winter activity?

   A. Snowball fight

   B. Sledding

   C. Ice skating

   D. Christmas shopping

2. The music that plays during the opening is the now-classic Christmas song "Christmas Time Is Here," composed by what famous jazz pianist?

   A. Vince Guaraldi

   B. Duke Ellington

   C. Count Basie

   D. Dave Brubeck

3. Lucy lets Charlie Brown know that there's a perfect time to eat snowflakes and that she would prefer to wait until what month for prime snowflake flavor?

   A. December

   B. January

   C. February

   D. March

Festive Fact

Charlie Brown's decision to choose a real tree instead of the aluminum one inspired consumers to do the same. After the special, aluminum Christmas tree sales began to decline.

4. Charlie Brown listens to Lucy complain about the fact that she never gets what she really wants for Christmas, as she lists off things she doesn't like. What does she really want?

   A. Toys

   B. Bicycle

   C. Clothes

   D. Real estate

5. After being threatened with a knuckle sandwich by Lucy, how is Linus allowed to keep his blanket while performing in the play?

   A. He pays her a nickel

   B. He hides it under his shirt

   C. He wears it as a hat

   D. He wears it as a cape

6. **No one agrees to it, but Schroeder proposes playing music from what classical artist for the Christmas play?**

    A. Beethoven

    B. Mozart

    C. Handel

    D. Bach

7. **Who wins the coveted first prize for Best Christmas Decorations in Town, much to the dismay of Charlie Brown?**

    A. Lucy

    B. Linus

    C. Pig-Pen

    D. Snoopy

8. **During the finale, when Charlie Brown's little Christmas tree is fully decorated (with help from everyone else), what song do all the Peanuts characters hum together?**

    A. "Hark! The Herald Angels Sing"

    B. "O Christmas Tree"

    C. "The Happiest Christmas Tree"

    D. "Joy to the World"

Arthur Christmas

Year: 2011

Director: Sarah Smith

Writers: Peter Baynham, Sarah Smith

Cast: James McAvoy, Hugh Laurie, Bill Nighy, Jim Broadbent, Imelda Staunton

Plot: When a technical glitch in the North Pole's modern and high-tech operations results in a little girl's Christmas present being missed, Santa's clumsy but well-meaning son Arthur embarks on an urgent mission to deliver it before sunrise.

Cheer-O-Meter

Christmas Spirit

Warm Fuzzies

Timelessness

1. Santa Claus is on his seventieth mission and has mostly been relegated to a figurehead, with his Elf Battalions and North Pole Mission Control running operations with military precision. What is the name of the high-tech ship that's replaced the sleigh and reindeer?

   A. SK-1

   B. K-1

   C. S-1

   D. Santa-1

Festive Fact

In the beginning of the film, the filmmakers pay homage to the iconic Alfred Eisenstaedt photo *V-J Day in Times Square*, with two elves standing in for the sailor and dental assistant for a perfectly timed kiss.

2. Steve, Santa's eldest son, who expects to take the reins after this latest Christmas, can usually be seen using what helpful device known as the HOHO 3000?

   A. Hydrographic Overt Home Office

   B. Handheld Operational and Homing Organizer

   C. High-Altitude Organizational Homing Organizer

   D. Hyperspectral Offshore Humanitarian Operation

3. After Christmas is considered "mission accomplished," one child does not get a gift delivered. Gwen Hines (47785BXK) wants a pink Twinkle Bike, and Arthur takes it upon himself to make sure she gets it. What part of England does Gwen live in?

   A. Trelew, Cornwall

   B. Brixham, Torbay

   C. Horfield, Bristol

   D. Canterbury, Kent

4. What is the name of the original wooden sleigh that was out of commission until Grandsanta accompanies Arthur to help him on his mission?

   A. E.L.F.

   B. JOY

   C. XMS

   D. EVE

Festive Fact

In a fun Easter egg, Steve, voiced by Hugh Laurie, has a goatee shaped like a Christmas tree.

5. Grandsanta pulls out an ancient map he used to guide the sleigh during his tenure. What is the name of this map of the world?

   A. The Reindeer Road Atlas

   B. The Christmas Constellation Compass

   C. The Map of the Clauses

   D. The Holiday Earth Atlas

6. Bryony Shelfley is an elf who stows away on the sleigh to help the cause. What is Bryony's specialty as an elf that helps them escape being attacked by lions in Africa?

   A. Wrapping

   B. Maintenance

   C. Building

   D. Repair

7. Grandsanta admits that this night is terrible, just like the last time he took the sleigh for a spin during what international incident?

   A. The stock market crash

   B. The sinking of the *Titanic*

   C. The Watergate scandal

   D. The Cuban Missile Crisis

8. What is the only thing that Arthur thinks he's good at, which helps him regain control of the rogue sleigh and reindeer flying around the world at supermassive speeds?

   A. Believing

   B. Worrying

   C. Ideating

   D. Scheming

How the Grinch Stole Christmas!

Cheer-O-Meter

Christmas Spirit

Warm Fuzzies

Timelessness

Year: 1966

Director: Chuck Jones, Ben Washam

Writers: Dr. Seuss, Irv Spector, Bob Ogle

Cast: June Foray, Dallas McKennon, Thurl Ravenscroft, MGM Studio Chorus

Plot: Based on the 1957 children's book of the same name, this iconic holiday special tells the story of the Grinch, a grumpy creature who attempts to ruin Christmas for the cheerful residents of Whoville.

1. What actor, horror icon, and former scientist's creation not only narrates the TV special but also provides the voice of the Grinch?

   A. Bela Lugosi

   B. Lon Chaney

   C. Boris Karloff

   D. Claude Rains

Festive Fact

This legendary performer who voices the Grinch was seventy-nine years old when he recorded the movie. His performance won him the only major award of his career: a children's recording Grammy.

2. During the Grinch's visions, he sees an annoyingly endless feast (that he can't stand in the least), where a parade of increasingly tiny waiters hidden in serving trays gives Cindy Lou Who what treat? The image of it dissolves into the pupil of the Grinch's eye.

   A. Beet

   B. Cherry

   C. Strawberry

   D. Watermelon

3. Just how long has the Grinch been dealing with the Who-Christmas-Sing before he decides enough is enough and he can't take it anymore?

   A. 53 years

   B. 33 years

   C. 63 years

   D. 23 years

4. The Grinch gets the idea to dress up like Santa from seeing his loyal companion, Max, with a snow beard. During a sewing montage, we hear Thurl Ravenscroft sing "You're a Mean One, Mr. Grinch," in which he sings that he wouldn't touch the Grinch with a pole that's how long?

   A. 35½ feet

   B. 39½ feet

   C. 36½ feet

   D. 33½ feet

5. At stop number one on his campaign to ruin Christmas, the Grinch slides down the chimney and decides which decoration is the first thing to go?

    A. Christmas wreaths

    B. Christmas tree

    C. Christmas lights

    D. Christmas stockings

6. When Cindy Lou Who asks the Grinch why he's taking her family's tree, what fib does he fool her with before patting her head, getting her a drink, and sending her to bed?

    A. He needs to trim the tree because it's grown too big

    B. He wants to add more ornaments to the tree

    C. He's taking it to his workshop to fix a light that won't work

    D. He wants to replace it with a new bigger and better one

7. At a quarter to dawn, the Grinch packs up his sleigh with all the stolen goods, and with help from Max submarining in the snow, the sleigh reaches a height of how many feet?

    A. 5,000

    B. 8,000

    C. 10,000

    D. 12,000

8. After the Grinch finds the strength of ten Grinches plus two, he brings back all the presents, decorations, and food for the feast. Who is the first attendee to get food?

   A. The Mayor of Whoville

   B. Max

   C. The Grinch

   D. Cindy Lou Who

Klaus

Year: 2019

Director: Sergio Pablos

Writers: Sergio Pablos, Jim Mahoney, Zach Lewis

Cast: Jason Schwartzman, J. K. Simmons, Rashida Jones, Will Sasso, Joan Cusack

Plot: In a new twist on Santa Claus's origins, a hapless postal academy student, Jesper, finds himself in a desolate, frozen village above the arctic circle, where he forms an unlikely friendship with a reclusive toymaker.

Cheer-O-Meter

Christmas Spirit

Warm Fuzzies

Timelessness

1. Jesper, the self-centered son of the Royal Postmaster General, is assigned to what far-off city, home of the world's finest feuds?

   A. Streetersburg

   B. Smeerensburg

   C. Slavisburg

   D. Stalinsburg

2. As Jesper tries to take over his new post office, what animals have set up shop and become his new roommates in the rickety building?

   A. Reindeer

   B. Rats

   C. Puffins

   D. Chickens

3. A reclusive woodsman and toy maker named Klaus initially scares Jesper away, but after finding Jesper's first letter, the bearded man enlists him to deliver what toy to a sad child in town?

   A. A pull-string frog

   B. A pull-string bunny

   C. A pull-string mouse

   D. A pull-string duck

Festive Fact

Klaus is the first animated film from Netflix to be nominated for an Academy Award.

4. Much of Santa's lore is created by accident throughout the course of the film. Which of the following did NOT lead to the Santa legend we now know and love?

   A. Jesper was called a loser and thus created the Naughty List

   B. Escaping an ambush, the sleigh hits a big hill and appears to a child to be flying

   C. Márgu's community inspires Klaus to wear all red

   D. Stockings became gift receptacles after Jesper hung out his wet socks to dry

5. Klaus reveals that the only reason he started making toys was for the children he and his wife planned on having but couldn't conceive. What is the name of Klaus's wife, who calls him back home at the end of the film?

   A. Lydia

   B. Linnea

   C. Lorelei

   D. Lillian

6. Teaming up with Jesper is Alva, a teacher whose classroom is always empty. She uses her life savings hidden in what location to fix up the school, revitalizing the town?

   A. In a birdhouse

   B. Under the floorboards

   C. In an igloo

   D. In the mouth of a dead fish

7. Márgu, who repeatedly visits Jesper to try to write a letter (despite not speaking English), asks for a sled that Klaus and Jesper work together to make. Márgu is a member of what Indigenous people?

   A. Inuit

   B. Maori

   C. Sámi

   D. Cree

8. An important theme of the film is something that Klaus always says rubs off on Jesper. Can you complete the poignant quote from the future Saint Nick? "A true act of goodwill _____."

   A. Goes a long way

   B. Makes hearts grow

   C. Never fades away

   D. Always sparks another

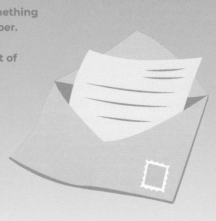

The Polar Express

Cheer-O-Meter

Christmas Spirit

Warm Fuzzies

Timelessness

Year: 2004

Director: Robert Zemeckis

Writers: Robert Zemeckis, William Broyles Jr.

Cast: Tom Hanks, Daryl Sabara, Nona Gaye, Jimmy Bennett, Eddie Deezen

Plot: A young boy skeptical of the magic of Christmas boards a mysterious and magical train known as the Polar Express headed for the North Pole.

1. When Hero Boy enters the train and takes his seat, he meets Know-It-All, a bespectacled and talkative kid who informs him that the train is a Baldwin 2-8-4 S3-class Berkshire-type steam locomotive. What type of design is on Know-It-All's pajamas?

   A. Jupiter Explorer rocket ship

   B. Periodic table of elements

   C. Nuclear radiation symbol

   D. Atoms and math equations

2. Served by an octet of singing and dancing waiters and two chefs, the Polar Express guarantees hot chocolate for all passengers if they follow what important rule?

   A. You can never have too many marshmallows

   B. Never ever let it cool

   C. Always drink it in a big mug

   D. The more chocolate, the better

3. When Hero Boy first sees the Hobo, he is by a fire with a hot cup of joe playing a hurdy-gurdy and humming what Christmas carol?

   A. "O Holy Night"

   B. "In the Bleak Midwinter"

   C. "Silent Night"

   D. "Good King Wenceslas"

4. Hero Boy has Hero Girl's lost ticket, which was caught up with a wolf pack, regurgitated by a baby eagle, and then turned into a snowball. The Hobo tells him to hide it in what safe place?

   A. His underwear

   B. His sock

   C. His shoe

   D. His pocket

5. The Polar Express is in some serious jelly when the engineer asks Hero Boy and Hero Girl to hit the brakes due to what kind of animal blocking the tracks?

   A. Polar bear

   B. Caribou

   C. Reindeer

   D. Penguin

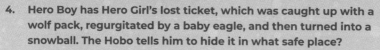

Festive Fact

Director Robert Zemeckis was inspired by his upbringing in Chicago for some of the look of the film. The address where Billy lives is 11344 Edbrooke Avenue, which was inspired by Robert Zemeckis's childhood home address.

6. **Thanks to a faulty cotter pin and no communication with the engineer, the Conductor, Hero Boy, and Hero Girl must hold on tightly as they accelerate uncontrollably toward what downhill grade, the steepest in the world?**

   A. Avalanche Alley

   B. Blizzard Bend

   C. Summit Slope

   D. Glacier Gulch

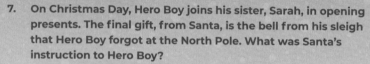

7. **On Christmas Day, Hero Boy joins his sister, Sarah, in opening presents. The final gift, from Santa, is the bell from his sleigh that Hero Boy forgot at the North Pole. What was Santa's instruction to Hero Boy?**

   A. Never forget me

   B. Be good to your sister

   C. Fix that hole in your pocket

   D. Make friends and cherish them

8. **Match the Polar Express passenger to the message punched on their golden ticket:**

1. BELIEVE	A. Billy
2. LEARN	B. Hero Boy
3. DEPEND ON, RELY ON, COUNT ON	C. Hero Girl
4. LEAD	D. Know-It-All

Santa's Workshop— How Did This Get Made?

Each year, Santa's elves and their massive workshop make everything from spinning tops to wooden horses to video-game systems and whatever else kids can dream up. Can you match these films with their origin stories?

1. *The Star* (2017)

2. *Christmas Comes but Once a Year* (1936)

3. *Yes, Virginia* (2009)

4. *Rise of the Guardians* (2012)

5. *Grandma Got Run Over by a Reindeer* (2000)

A. Based on a 1979 novelty Christmas song written by Randy Brooks and most famously performed by Elmo & Patsy

B. Based on the Nativity of Jesus and features voice work from Steven Yeun, Keegan-Michael Key, Gina Rodriguez, and Zachary Levi

C. Made by famed animation house Fleischer Studios and features the character known as Professor Grampy (a character from Betty Boop)

D. Based on perhaps the most famous newspaper editorial response in history by Francis Pharcellus Church in the New York newspaper *The Sun* on September 21, 1897

E. Adapted from a series of successful books by William Joyce that feature reimagined versions of the Sandman, the Tooth Fairy, the Easter Bunny, and Jack Frost

POST-CREDITS

⭐ *The Polar Express* is based on the children's picture book of the same name written and illustrated by Chris Van Allsburg, who received the Caldecott Medal for his illustrations in the book.

⭐ Real children were cast in the roles in *A Charlie Brown Christmas*. The filmmakers soon realized that several of the children (like Christopher Shea, who voiced Linus) couldn't read the script, so Charles Schulz and director Bill Melendez had to recite the script to them line by line.

⭐ *Arthur Christmas* was made by Aardman Animations Limited, a British animation studio based in Bristol, England, known for their stop-motion and clay-animation *Wallace and Gromit* series.

Stocking Stuffer

A Rankin/Bass Christmas

It's time to celebrate arguably the two most important names in Christmas history: Arthur Rankin Jr. and Jules Bass. This illustrious duo of animators, known for their unique animation style called "Animagic" (along with animation pioneer Tadahito "Tad" Mochinaga), are responsible for an iconic catalog of holiday specials including *Rudolph the Red-Nosed Reindeer*, *Santa Claus Is Comin' to Town*, and *Frosty the Snowman*—all beloved by generations and woven into the very fabric of the holiday season.

'Twas the Night Before Christmas (1974)

Human clockmaker Joshua Trundle and his assistant, Father Mouse, build what special apparatus to convince Santa Claus to stop in their town of Junctionville after he is offended by an anonymous letter to the newspaper claiming he didn't exist?

Frosty the Snowman (1969)

Frosty can speak, he can move, he can juggle, sweep, and count to five. Thanks to Professor Hinkle's magic hat, what were his first words after coming alive?

Jack Frost (1979)

What fake identity (the name being an onomatopoeia that fits well in a tailor shop) does Jack adopt when Father Winter makes him human, allowing him to woo Elisa, the girl he rescues from Kubla Kraus and falls in love with?

Nestor, the Long-Eared Christmas Donkey (1977)

What first name is shared between this film's cruel stable owner, who mistreats Nestor and throws him out into a blizzard, and the equally cold animated character from a Disney blockbuster, who famously says, "Some people are worth melting for"?

Rudolph the Red-Nosed Reindeer (1964)

What is the name of the winged feline ruler of the Island of Misfit Toys who greets Rudolph, Hermey, and Yukon Cornelius? (If you drop the C and add a K, you'd get James Bond in space with an equally toothy abominable antagonist.)

Santa Claus Is Comin' to Town (1970)

What famous actor lent his voice and Funny Face to the character of Special Delivery Kluger (or S.D. for short), the postman and narrator of the film, who tells the origins of Santa Claus and how he got his powers from the Winter Warlock?

The First Christmas: The Story of the First Christmas Snow (1975)

Three nuns named Sister Catherine, Sister Jean, and Sister Theresa (voiced by Angela Lansbury, who narrates) take in a young shepherd named Lucas, who sustains what injury from a lightning strike a few weeks before Christmas?

The Life and Adventures of Santa Claus (1985)

This television special is based on the 1902 children's book of the same name by what author, who traded in the yellow brick road for snowy woods and the Forest of Burzee?

The Little Drummer Boy (1968)

Based on the song of the same name written by Katherine Kennicott Davis in 1941 (which was first recorded by the Trapp family, who were portrayed in *The Sound of Music*), this film gives the titular percussionist what first name?

The Year Without a Santa Claus (1974)

Mrs. Claus assigns two elves named Jingle and Jangle to find some much-needed Christmas spirit in Southtown because Santa Claus (voiced by Mickey Rooney) wants to cancel Christmas for what small but very relatable reason?

ANSWERS: 1. Singing clock tower, 2. "Happy Birthday!" 3. Jack Snip, 4. Olaf, 5. King Moonracer, 6. Fred Astaire, 7. Blindness, 8. L. Frank Baum, 9. Aaron, 10. He has a cold

Film Index

(in alphabetical order)

Acknowledgments

Thank you to my wife, Colleen, who watched every movie with me. Like George Bailey, I'll never stop trying to give you the moon. To my own Griswold clan: Tom, Kathy, David, Maxwell, Jim, Marge, Fafa, Hank, and Dina, there's nobody else I'd rather be in misery with on Christmas. And to Aria and Ivy, sorry I didn't include *Frozen*. But it's not a Christmas movie. If you're sad, I hope one day you let it go.

To Justin Brouckaert of Aevitas Creative Management, the most dashing man in Detroit (who doesn't rap about mom's spaghetti), thanks for being the Sergeant Al Powell to my John McClane and for always being on the other side of the radio.

For guiding this paper-backed sleigh of trivia goodness, thank you to Kristin Mehus-Roe and Leah Tracosas Jenness for your edits, ideas, infectious enthusiasm, and Christmas joy. Cara Donaldson, Tim Palin, Tiffany Taing, Nick Allison, and the entire Quarto team, thank you for all your hard work. I'm proud to have my name on this cover and will triple-dog-dare anyone to convince me otherwise. Gratitude also to Lori Burke, for being so welcoming to a pop culture nerd like me, and Nicole James for opening the door to the North Pole in the first place.

Like Ernest, the following people also saved Christmas and presumably love denim: Phil, Shady, Erica, Vicki, James, Kim, Kirch, Walling, Ede, Markkus, Barber, Ryan Meyers, Matt Kirk, the gents at *The Benchwarmers Trivia Podcast*, Julia and Lauren of the *Miss Information* podcast, Jay from Liquid Kourage Entertainment, the staff of Blackberry Market, and Gosia's Coffee Shop, anyone who filled out the cheer-o-meter form, friends, family, listeners, supporters, and anyone who received texts and messages from me asking, "Does this make sense?" And one more thanks to Mom and Dad for always spoiling us and never failing to make it the hap-hap-happiest Christmas.